MONEY
PRESENT AND FUTURE

CREATING THE PATH TO TURNING MONEY INTO YOUR
ALLY TO ACHIEVE RESIDUAL INCOME IN YOUR LIFE.

PATRIC CHAN

Internet Mastermind Sdn Bhd

Correspondence Address:
1-3-22 eGate Commercial Complex, Lebuh Tunku Kudin 2,
11700 Penang.
Email: rep@masterminddotcom.com

ISBN 979-885-49081-8-4

DISCLAIMER: This publication provides competent and reliable information regarding the subject covered. However, it is sold understanding that the authors and publisher are not engaged in rendering legal, financial or other expert assistance is required, the services of the professional should be sought. The authors and publisher specifically disclaim any liability incurred from the user or application of the contents of this book.

To my wife, Emily…

My 3 children – Marin, Marireis and Reeve…

I love you so much.

Contents

About The Author

Despite his humble beginnings as the son of a taxi driver, Patric Chan has risen to international acclaim as a highly respected author and internet marketing pioneer, starting in 2004. Born and raised on a small island in Penang, Patric didn't have a traditional educational path. He didn't attend university or college, and when he first ventured into the global market, his English was far from fluent compared to today's.

But none of these challenges deterred him.

Equipped with an unwavering determination and a deep-seated passion for entrepreneurship, Patric set out to create his future. His journey is a testament to his credo that everyone, regardless of their past or present circumstances, can achieve greatness if they have the will to strive for it.

To date, Patric Chan is a best-selling author of multiple books, including co-author a book with Robert G. Allen, and an international speaker of 12 countries in the United States, China, Australia, the UK, Singapore and others.

He has been featured in newspapers many times and also in business magazines. Patric has taught his techniques and strategies to thousands of his students through his books, courses, seminars and live training.

He is also the mastermind behind the innovative Operation Zero Employees model. This revolutionary approach empowers marketers and entrepreneurs to build and operate digital businesses without needing a traditional team of employees.

This system has not only brought Patric immense success but has also given him the freedom to balance his professional goals with his personal life.

Testimonials from ordinary people whose lives he has touched and from international best-selling authors and millionaires speak volumes about Patric's impact. His primary focus today is helping ordinary people and marketers to create freedom. Patric leverages his expertise for business owners to help them achieve 2x to 10x breakthroughs in their current earnings.

As a proud father of three, Patric deeply values his time with his family. His children are a constant source of joy and motivation for him.

Despite his accomplishments, Patric remains down-to-earth and approachable. He is known for his dedication to his students and ability to simplify complex concepts. Patric Chan's journey continues to inspire and guide those who aspire to create their own path in the digital business world, proving that anyone can achieve financial freedom with determination, creativity, and the right strategies.

To connect with Patric:

Facebook, https://fb.com/patricchanlive
YouTube, https://youtube.com/patricchan
TikTok, https://tiktok.com/patricchan
IG, https://instagram.com/officialpatricchan
Telegram, https://t.me/officialpatricchan
Podcast. https://pod.co/patric
Website, https://patricchan.com

Introduction: Why Write Another Book About Money

I don't want to write another motivational book about money. Or wealth. There are already plenty of these books, easily hundreds that are good. Then, of course, there are thousands on this topic to motivate you to become rich.

And this is definitely different from a financial planning book.

The reason why I wrote this book is for my children.

In 2019, there was a video of Logan Paul interviewing a kid who was 15 years old at that time. That kid's name is Jack Doherty. At that time, while he was just a kid, he bought his own house. He was making 6 figures in income from YouTube, maybe even hitting a million dollars.

Anyway, the exciting story is about more than just making so much money - But having the financial education about MONEY and how he had learned to invest at a young age.

If he has that knowledge, I doubt he'll have any challenges in achieving financial freedom later in his life.

Because at the same time, many kids, such as young actors, amass much money, yet they become poor in their adult life.

That made me curious about financial independence in our society today.

What if...

I can teach my children about money while they're still schooling...

Wouldn't it be amazing if they had a stable income stream before they even completed their studies in colleges or universities?

This way, when they want to start working, they can pick a job they would be interested in instead of choosing a job based on how much they can earn from the salary.

That's why I'm writing MONEY: Present And Future.

It's a self-serving reason. Really.

And in my opinion, if I'm confident the information in the book can transform my children's life, why should I be selfish and keep it from others?

The fact is, for adults too.

To me, unless you're already 70, then perhaps there's nothing much this book could do to change your financial situation. And ironically, money should not even be on your priority list to attain at this age bracket (unless you're in a dire state).

Because if you have your hands on this book before it's too late, you can still create the path to living with money happily.

Meaning money would not burden you anymore.

Because money DOES affect everything in your life.

Want to have a better relationship?

Having money helps because you can need to trade time for money and use your available time to spend it with someone you like or care about.

Health?

Of course. Less trading time for money would mean you'll have more time to participate in exercises and even sleep more.

Money will also allow you to get supplements for your body's nutrients.

YES – many things in life, especially happiness, can be attained without money.

But why refuse the rest of the happiness that can be gained with money as the leverage to attain?

So what's MONEY: Present And Future going to be about?

Quite simple.

It'll be based on my personal experience with money.

The mistakes I've made to lose money.

The correct approaches to money have helped me to be debt-free.

Here's the fact:

If I had known all of these, all of the knowledge in this book, I would:

- I have made more money at my age today.

- Built a giant pipe of passive income

I would have achieved what I've achieved today, maybe in my 30's. I'm now in my 40's, meaning I would have about ten years of more enjoyment.

This book is written as a playbook, a guide to help someone never have a lack of money in his life ever.

And it's called "present and future" because for us to have a bright future with money, never to have the lack of it, we must first fix the "present" and lay the foundation for the future.

At the same time, please don't treat this book as financial. I cover some discussions about stocks and cryptos, but this is not an investment book. I'm not an investment guru.

You don't need to follow my advice either, as I don't claim to be correct.

The playbook here is right for me – maybe, it's suitable for my lifestyle and my goals in life.

You don't need to follow my advice either, as I don't claim to be correct. It may even contradict those "how to be rich" or self-help books out there simply because MONEY: Present

And Future is not based on what I read, it's just based on my experience with money. And I'm debt-free today.

For me, money is a tool to attain what you want in life that can lead to living abundantly, being contented and happy; money should not be a yardstick of success.

I hope you'll enjoy reading the book.

The Psychology of Money

The psychology of money is all about our beliefs and emotions connected to it. Even though money isn't a living thing and we can't hurt its feelings, our views and feelings about money are strong.

Whether people become rich or not is about more than just their skill in earning (and keeping) money. It's about their psychology around money — their views of it, how they treat it, what money means to them, and more.

Money Is Emotional

Let's talk about how money stirs up our feelings.

We all know money isn't alive. It doesn't breathe, it doesn't eat, and it definitely doesn't have feelings. But we humans?

We get all emotional about it. Money's not just a bunch of numbers on a screen or a piece of paper to us. It's something that can make us jump for joy or lose sleep.

It's a symbol that can evoke feelings ranging from joy to anxiety.

In my own company, I always tell my team that if a customer double-buys our product or asks for a refund, sort it out quickly. I'm talking light-speed. Why? Because I get how people feel about their money.

I've seen that customers can get anxious about their cash. If they ask for a refund and don't hear back within an hour, they'll be right back to you with another email.

It's not a bad thing, but it sure can be dramatic. And customers who are super attached to their money? Those can be tough to deal with. But hey, this isn't about running a business. It's about understanding how we feel about money.

Think about this…

You've got a $50 bill. To you, it's just 50 bucks. But to someone else, it could be a whole different story. If you're pulling in $10,000 a month, spending $500 on a product, 50 bucks is a slight change. But what if that's the last bit of money someone's got in their account?

How much money means to you can shape how you feel about it. And those feelings? They're going to guide your choices about earning or saving.

If you cultivate a negative association with money, it can impact you adversely. For instance, if you treat money as being "too valuable," you may become overly frugal. This could lead to avoiding outings with friends; you might find yourself alone over time.

Similarly, viewing money as a "scarce" resource could make you fearful of investing due to the risk of loss.

You may start seeing money as a rare gem that's hard to come by. Then you might become too scared to invest because you don't want to lose what little you have.

So here's the thing: money and emotions are tied together. But what kind of feelings are you letting money stir up in you?

Don't let your emotions take the driver's seat when dealing with money. Most of the time, if you make decisions based on how you feel rather than thinking them through, you will regret it.

When handling your money, leave your feelings out because managing money wisely should not be about emotion.

It should be based on logic and proper planning.

Money's Value: Unchanged and Unaffected

Let's have a straight talk about money.

Consider a $50 note again.

It's worth 50 bucks, right? No more, no less.

But here's where it gets tricky: that same $50 note can feel different depending on who's holding it.

This is what I find utterly fascinating. The face value of money, it's constant. It doesn't matter who you are, how much you have in the bank, or how you feel about it. A $50 note is still worth $50 whether you're a millionaire or living paycheck to paycheck. The value of money, it just doesn't change. It remains unaffected by our personal circumstances.

Now, some might think that having more money in the bank somehow reduces the worth of that $50 note. But here's the truth. Whether you have $500 or $1,000,000, that $50 note doesn't change its value. It's still worth $50.

Let's consider an example. An employee gets his paycheck and feels rich. The first week, he spends freely, not realizing that his money is dwindling. He might spend $200 on a meal and drinks, thinking it's a little since he still has $9,800 left. But the truth is, spending $200 is a lot, regardless of how much he has left.

Similarly, an entrepreneur who makes a hefty profit might start paying more for things, overspending without realizing it. Because he has more money, he might perceive the value of it as less. But in reality, the value of money hasn't changed. He's just spending it more freely.

So, here's the critical point. Understanding that the value of money remains constant is the key to using it wisely.

If you think having more money makes it less valuable and leads you to spend more, then you've got it all wrong. This mindset can lead to overspending and poor financial decisions.

Remember, it's not just about how much money you have.

It's about understanding its value and using it wisely. So, don't let your emotions or the money you have in your bank account to cloud your judgment. Make your decisions based on the actual value of money and good planning.

That's the secret to making your money work for you later on.

Money Is An Attractor

Look, I'm blessed to have friends who don't care whether I have money or not. Why? Because they were there for me before I had money.

But take a good look around you, and you'll realize that money does have a strange ability to attract people into your circle.

Similarly, money can pull you towards others. Don't get me wrong; I'm not talking about romantic attraction. I'm talking about general attraction, like a magnet. It just... attracts.

But here's the thing you need to keep in mind. If you want to live happily with money without constantly being in lack, you need to surround yourself with folks who share the same principles.

Now, if you're not smart about your money, you'll end up attracting two types of people: those who are equally careless about their finances or those who are just waiting to take advantage of your lack of wisdom.

In my humble opinion, using money to gain friends is the worst way. I mean, think about it. If you're always flaunting shiny objects on social media to get attention, who are you attracting, really?

You're just inviting people who are drawn to the glitter rather than the person behind it.
Conversely, you'll attract like-minded people if you're smart with your money. You'll likely spend wisely because when you hang out with them, they're not the type to splurge more than they can afford.

Here's another cool thing about the psychology of money. If you're good at making money, more money will come to you. It's a weird law of nature that money attracts money.

So, what's your job?

Well, it's to ensure you're on the right side of the attraction.

Money Is Always Moving

Did you know that, according to the U.S. Bureau of Economic Analysis, personal consumption expenditures (PCE) hit around $14.96 trillion in 2020?

If you break it down, that's about $41 billion getting passed around daily. We're sticking to 2020's numbers for now since I couldn't find more recent data. But think about it - $41 billion is being exchanged daily.

What does this mean? Simple. There's always someone selling something, and there's always someone else buying it. No exception.

If you're constantly asking yourself, "How can I make more money," you're asking the wrong question. And that could be why you're not reaching your goals.

Here's the thing…

There's no such thing as "making" more money. The money is already here.

As you're reading this, millions of dollars are changing hands. The unfortunate part is that those millions aren't landing in your hands.

So, what's your job? It's to divert that flow of money to you - legally, of course.

Stop asking yourself how to make money. Start asking yourself what you can do to deserve that money.

I made my money by building businesses. So, for a business to be successful, it has to sell something. That means my job is to be good at selling.

But if you dig deeper, the core strategy to divert the flow of money to you is to provide value to someone else.

I've trained thousands of students to earn income from the Internet, and unfortunately, most failed. It's not something I'm embarrassed about because it has little to do with my teachings or coaching. I've given them marketing and business knowledge but can't change their mindset.

You see, most people are always thinking about how they can make money instead of focusing on delivering value. My successful students, the ones who have successfully generated income on the internet, are focusing on selling products or services that customers want to buy. They're not trying to "make money online."

Does the idea of trying to "catch" moving money seem stressful? Well, let's look at it another way.

Consider an experienced fisherman. He consistently comes home with a bountiful catch.

How?

Because he knows where to fish and the best times to cast his line. But acquiring this valuable knowledge probably involved several failures. Yet, because he learned from those experiences, he knows how the fish "move."

The initial stages are typically the most challenging. But pause for a moment and think... have you ever met a self-made millionaire or highly successful entrepreneur who hadn't faced hardships when they first started? Ask them if it was worth navigating those "stressful thoughts," and you'll likely be met with a knowing smile.

The truth is that there are shortcuts to wealth and success, and knowledge is one of them.

Money In Abundance

Let's pick up from where we left off in the previous chapter. We talked about money constantly flowing, right?

Now, let's talk about another awesome thing about money. It's abundant. I mean, seriously plentiful. So much, in fact, that technically, money will never run out.

Ever think about how our financial system works?

Banks, investment firms, and stock exchanges are like these massive engines constantly churning out opportunities. They help people manage, invest, and multiply their money. They make it possible for folks like you and me to borrow, lend, invest, and create wealth.

Here's an excellent way to visualize it. Imagine a river, constantly flowing, always providing. That's money. Now, compare that to a rare gem in a mountain. That gem is finite; once it's gone, it's gone. But the river? It keeps on flowing.

Money is like that river, not the gem. Money is here, there, everywhere.

This leads us to ponder this…

If money were a rare commodity like diamonds, it wouldn't matter how hard you worked; you couldn't just create more diamonds. But with money, it's a whole different ballgame. If you know, there's always a supply of money available that can change your entire approach. It means that if you put in the work, there's always the possibility of earning more. That thought alone can really fuel your fire.

But that doesn't means it'll be available for you whenever you want – you need to start early.

Now, here's a reality check. As we grow older, we might lose some advantages. It's a bit harsh, but that's how the game is played. It's not about being fair or unfair - it's about knowing the rules and playing to win.

You might wonder why being young gives you an edge in making money. Don't worry. We're going to delve deep into that topic in later chapters. But here's a sneak peek: when you're young, you have time on your side. You have the luxury of time to learn, make mistakes, bounce back, and still have plenty of time to build and enjoy your wealth.

So, there you have it. Money's abundant. It's like that river, constantly flowing, always providing.

Spending Money At Present

The first step on our journey is to grasp the psychology of money. It's essential to set the right mindset towards it.

Here's something that might surprise you...

Even intelligent people can lose money if they have a rocky "relationship" with it.

Imagine money as your ally helping you achieve your life goals, not an obstacle standing in your way.

Sure, there are countless books out there teaching you about money. But I want to focus on the earlier four psychological aspects that have truly made a difference for me and have proven their worth in practice.

I don't aim to feed you theoretical concepts but to share what has worked for me.

Once our mindset is in check, it's time to dive into the science of using and earning money.

Becoming wealthy and achieving financial freedom means tackling any present issues head-on whereas motivational books usually skip this part. They are focused on inspiring you to be rich, not necessarily guiding you on how to get there.

So, the first part of our present journey is ensuring you're not veering off track.

Once you've dodged the wrong steps, it's time to implement the right ones. Ready to start this journey? Let's dive in...

Your Spending Must Be Less Than You Earn

When I was a fresh-faced twenty-something, I launched my first company. The business model was straightforward - partner with a talented speaker and promote him. We sold workshop seats and earned money.

Then one day, out of the blue, the bank manager called me.

"Mr. Chan," he said, "your cheque bounced." I was taken aback. I was sure of my earnings.

I mean, if each seat sold for 2K, selling 25 seats would net me 50K, right? It was simple math.

The reality, though, was harsh. I was spending more than I was earning. This poor cash management eventually led to the downfall of my company. Only then did I dive into the world of internet marketing.

Now, let me clarify something...

It wasn't that I was splurging left, right, and center. I was just paying vendors and salaries as per the business needs. But as they say, the devil is in the details, and the fact I overlooked was my spending.

This is why I'm dedicating an entire chapter to this topic.

Many people fall into the trap of poor money management without even realizing it.

The cardinal rule of money management is this - if you earn 1K, do not spend 1K.

I know the temptation to splurge is strong, especially when you start earning. But hold your horses. The time to spend freely will come when you're not living paycheck to paycheck. For now, patience is the key. Trust me; it'll be worth the wait.

See, I learned the hard way. If you don't respect this cardinal rule, you're heading straight for debt. And let me tell you, debt is the bogeyman of financial freedom. It's the antithesis of wealth.

To me, being in debt is equivalent to being broke.

It means you can't afford the finer things in life anymore.

And don't even get me started on the "good debt" versus "bad debt" debate. I don't buy it. To me, debt is just that - debt. I never want to be beholden to a debtor.

In my book, you're either free or you're not. And debt certainly doesn't spell freedom.

Spending less than you earn gives you flexibility and alleviates financial stress. You can step off the paycheck-to-paycheck treadmill that most salaried workers are stuck on. This financial cushion allows you to handle unexpected life events or changes in circumstances easily.

While this won't make you rich, it's the most straightforward action you can take to have more money and fewer worries.

So, how do you go about it?

Step 1: Assess Your Current Income

First, you need to take a comprehensive look at your income, expenses, and financial obligations. A clear understanding of your financial situation will tell you what you can afford and what you can't.

Step 2: Prioritize Needs Over Wants

Next, distinguish between essential needs and discretionary wants. Cover your necessary expenses first. You can indulge your desires if you still have money left over from the 80% of your income.

Step 3: Cut Further Expenses and Reduce Discretionary Spending

Now, comb through your list again. I bet you'll find more expenses that you can cut. For example, I changed my mobile plan to a more affordable one because I realized I didn't need that much data.

Another example: I used to have a house cleaner come in five days a week. One day, she fell ill and couldn't come in for two days. To my surprise, my house remained as clean as ever. I realized then that I didn't need daily cleaning services. Three days a week were enough to keep my house tidy. This change alone saved me two days' worth of cleaning fees.

You can also reduce your discretionary spending. For instance, you could downgrade your Netflix subscription to a cheaper package. Believe me; you won't notice the difference between 4K and HD quality on your TV.

If you're a drinker, consider cutting back. If you typically have five drinks, try having just four. You'll cut your drinking expenses by 20%.

Now, let me be clear. I'm not asking you to compromise your lifestyle. What's the point of earning money if you can't enjoy the basics of life, right?

What I'm suggesting is cutting unnecessary expenses. Spend wisely, and you can still enjoy the things you love without breaking the bank.

So, do you think you can tame the spending beast? It's a challenge, but the rewards are worth it.

The 3 Buckets Of Money Allocation

Your income should go into 3 buckets. For the context of it, your income is defined by the money you earn. Sometimes, you earn money elsewhere, not just your salary.

The 3 buckets are:

i. Savings that are safe all the time but have minimal return.
ii. Low-risk investments that are safe in the long run.
iii. High-risk investments but high returns.

Savings That Are Safe All The Time But Have Minimal Return

I'm not a financial planner, and this book is not about financial planning. My definition of this bucket is mostly for emergencies and predictable returns.

At the same time, I'm not a big fan of "saving to be rich". I believe that to be rich; you must learn how to acquire money rapidly and in mass. But you must have passive and semi-passive incomes to stop getting pressure from work.

I don't believe in retiring, either. I will still work, but not because of chasing money. Like writing this book. It's a form of "work," but regardless of whether this book makes money for me, I couldn't be bothered. I enjoy the work of being a creator (creating content) and being a teacher.

So, as a benchmark, you should have savings that can last you for six months without any incoming income. Then, continue to build that up to 12 months, etc. The more extended period you can build up your reserve, the happier person you'll be because you won't have financial stress. For me, I would like to have savings for three years.

Now that you understand the philosophy of it, let's plan out the allocation:

Initially, your allocation to savings would be higher than low-risk and high-risk investments.

Because you're building up your emergency portfolio, remember?

Once you hit the 6-month reserve, you can start different allocations.

To make sure we're on the same page:

The purpose of a "reserve" is to give you the time to recoup back your earnings if some financial catastrophe happens in your life. The concept of the Savings in this bucket is not for you to retire. So, the more months of reserve you have, the lesser your stress is going to be for you.

But here's the good news: You can still make your savings earn for you.

The common place for savings would be fixed deposits by banks. It's 100% safe unless the bank goes bust. And if you're ever afraid that such an incident may happen, use your country's national bank. That's very safe. However, I'll usually not go for fixed deposits because it's usually extremely low return (unless you can get a good interest rate).

At the same time, if you're young and working with a company, forced savings should also be initiated for you. Of course, different countries have different rules. I believe that in the US, it's called the 401(k) Employee Savings Plan. In Malaysia, it's called EPF.

I can't say for the US because I do not know the interest rates there, but here's my advice – you want to ensure your contributions to your employee saving plan never get interrupted.

I did not include it in the savings bucket simply because this kind of fund doesn't allow you to withdraw for emergencies (when you need the money immediately).

I don't want you to touch this fund because interests are being given out, and you're getting the compounding effect...

Compounding interest is a concept that refers to the ability of money to grow exponentially over time. It occurs when you earn interest on both your initial investment (principal) and the accumulated interest from previous periods. In simple terms, it means earning interest on top of interest.

For example, you invest $1,000 in a savings account with an annual interest rate of 5%. At the end of the first year, you would earn $50 in interest, bringing your total balance to $1,050. In the second year, the 5% interest is calculated on the new balance of $1,050, resulting in an additional $52.50. Over time, as the interest compounds, the snowball effect occurs, and your money grows faster and faster.

This compounding effect becomes more pronounced the longer you let your money grow, where the power of compounding lies in time. The earlier you start saving when you start working in a job, the more time your money has to compound and grow.

After all, the minimal income from your salary for your retirement plan savings won't make much difference in your lifestyle. But when you can withdraw it, the sum suddenly appears vast!

The other financial instrument for "Savings That Are Safe All The Time But Have Minimal Return" would be bonds.

You can easily inquire about bonds from your bank, but basically, this is what bonds investment is:

A bond is like a loan you give to a company or government. In return for your money, they promise to pay you interest at regular intervals and give back your original amount after a certain period. It's like lending money to a friend, and in return, they give you a little extra as a thank-you over time, and eventually, they'll pay you back the original amount you lent them.

Imagine you have a friend named Tim. Tim asks to borrow $100 from you, and in return, he promises to give you $5 every year as a small 'thank you' for the next 5 years. At the end of the 5 years, he'll give back your original $100. In this scenario, you're the bondholder, and Tim is like the company or government issuing the bond. The $5 he gives you annually is the interest, and the $100 he returns at the end is the bond's face value.

From here, I'll also split into 2 types of "savings" –

Type 1: Predictable Savings. This one would be such as fixed deposits, bonds, employee savings funds, etc. as explained earlier. The interest rate is fixed; thus, your return is predictable.

Type 2: Volatile Savings. For this one, my savings goes into investing in company shares that pay out dividends. While the interest return is not fixed, your return could also be higher.

A company dividend is a portion of the company's profits that is given to the shareholders. If you own shares in a company, you are one of its owners, and when the company makes money, they might decide to share some of that profit with you. It's like getting a slice of the pie from the profits that the company makes.

Imagine you and your friends decide to start a lemonade stand together. You all put in the work, and at the end of the day, you make a profit from selling lemonade. You then decide to divide the profit equally among yourselves. Each friend's share of the profit is like a company's dividend to its shareholders. If the lemonade stand is the company, then you and your friends are the shareholders, and the money you each take home at the end of the day is the dividend. It's your reward for being part of the business and helping it succeed.

But – instead of putting in your work, you're just an investor by buying the company's share.

There are companies that will pay out dividends each year, and some of them have higher returns than Type 1: Predictable Savings.

However, it's considered "volatile" simply because you could earn lesser or even none if the company did not perform well.

Usually, stocks from banks will have dividends.

For choosing a company that pays out dividends, the best bet is to choose an industry where it's "stable" and also "recession-proof" so that you can reduce unwanted surprises.

Once you've built up your reserve, I'll allocate between 40% - 50% towards the "Savings That Are Safe All The Time But Have Minimal Return" bucket.

This means if opportunity prevails in the other 2 buckets, I can reduce this bucket's portfolio to 40% but nothing less.

If you have $10, then $4 needs to be in this bucket to keep you not worried about money.

So what's the return I'm looking at?

Any "Savings" investment that gives 5% to 10% annual return.

Low-Risk Investments That Are Safe In The Long Run

For the remaining income that you have, after putting 40% or 50% into the saving bucket, the allocation for this would be 30% - 40%.

Here's how it works:

Assuming you already have your reserve, be it a 6-month reserve or a 3-year reserve. Whichever makes you feel comfortable (and also, depending on your age).

If this is my portfolio, 50% of my investment will go into the "Savings," and 40% could go into the "Low-Risk Investments That Are Safe In The Long Run" bucket.

But if you're more adventurous and begin to take higher risks, you can allocate just 30% here, and the rest goes to the "High-Risk Investments But High Return" bucket (the third bucket).

I can't teach you how to invest because that's not my expertise. As in, I can't direct you to where you should be investing. I'm just able to give you the guidelines.

Anyway, for this bucket, I'll consider the stock market.

I prefer the US stock market, which is often considered one of the leading stock markets in the world due to several factors that contribute to its prominence.

Size and Market Capitalization. The US stock market is the largest in the world regarding market capitalization. It is home to some of the largest and most valuable companies globally, such as Apple, Microsoft, Amazon, and Alphabet (Google). The size of the US market makes it an attractive destination for investors seeking exposure to companies with significant market presence and potential for growth.

In terms of this, the possibility of the company to grow tremendously is also high. Thus, the share price could also go many times fold over time.

A classic example would be Amazon, which went public in May 1997 with an initial public offering (IPO) price of $18 per share. The stock price closed its first day of trading at $23.05 per share, a gain of 25%.

In 2016, when Amazon's stock price was trading at $900 per share, Cathie Wood, the founder of ARK Invest, bought 1 million company shares. As of March 8, 2023, those 1 million shares would be worth over $3 billion.

Since then, Amazon's stock price has grown by an incredible amount. Based on March 8 2023, the stock price is $3,122.44 per share, a gain of over 17,000%.

There are a few reasons for Amazon's stock price growth.

First, the company has been a dominant force in the e-commerce market as the world's largest online retailer and has continued to grow its market share in recent years.

Second, Amazon has diversified its business beyond e-commerce. The company offers many products and services, including cloud computing, digital streaming, and artificial intelligence. This diversification has helped Amazon to reduce its reliance on e-commerce and improve its overall financial performance.

Third, Amazon has been investing heavily in growth. The company has spent billions of dollars on new warehouses, data centers, and other infrastructure. This investment has helped Amazon to keep up with demand and expand its reach into new markets.

I brought this up with some explanation of the company's background because I want you to understand this –

You'll choose the company's share to invest based on research, not by luck or listening to rumours.

I'll go for tech companies because I understand this industry better.

For instance, I would think Meta would be successful in the future despite all kinds of negative points about the company.

It may not be now, but a 10-year plan because I foresee that the growth of virtual reality and augmented reality will reach the mass by then and be adopted. If Meta's going to be the leading company in that space, why wouldn't the company's share be worth a lot then?

So, here is some of my advice for this bucket:

If you invest in a company's share, choose the industry you're familiar with and understand the company's product.

Always go for blue-chip companies. This bucket is not meant for high risk; with a blue-chip company, it's likely to survive any abnormality, also known as Black Swan events.

Choose the company for the FUTURE. Whether the company's product will always be in demand in the future or it's involved in the future's technology/product.

You're investing for the long term, expecting five years or more.

You're not supposed to "manage" this bucket. Meaning, in general, if the share price drops drastically, you're not supposed to let it go but buy more for averaging it out with the expectation that, over the years, it'll bounce back and continue to grow because of what the company's doing.

It'll also help you take some time to read about "fundamental investing". You're investing based on the company's performance and its future to grow, not based on the current sentiment or any stock charts.

Last but not least, for this second bucket, you're investing in the company's stocks for capital gain, not for dividends.

Because company stocks that have dividends usually don't have much capital gain and vice versa – companies with high capital gains do not perform well with dividends at all. Most of the time, there are zero dividends because the earnings of the company are usually re-invest into the company to continue expanding.

So what is capital gain?

It is the increase in the value of your investment. If you buy a stock at one price and later sell it for a higher price, the difference in the amount is your capital gain. Basically, it's the profit you make from selling your stock for more than you bought it for.

Imagine you buy a toy car for $10. Over time, this toy becomes popular and rare. A year later, someone offers you $20 for that same toy car. If you decide to sell it, you've made a profit of $10. This extra money you earned is like the capital gain in stock investment. Just as you sold your toy car for more than you bought it, you sell your stock for more than its original price.

For instance, with the Amazon stock's track record, I shared earlier. The capital gain was very impressive.

High-Risk Investments But High Return

The third bucket will be higher risk, but the return on investment (ROI) could be higher than the former.

At the same time, you should never gamble. Keep in mind that you're investing, not gambling, with your hard-earned income.

Gambling would mean you're "investing" without proper research or a plan.

For this bucket, I suggest investing in cryptos.

Of course, there's a massive debate about this in the investment world.

Warren Buffett, the legendary investor and CEO of Berkshire Hathaway, has been a vocal critic of cryptocurrencies like Bitcoin. Buffett's main objection to cryptocurrencies is that they do not produce anything of value. He compares them to tulip bulbs, once seen as a valuable investment but ultimately worthless. Buffett believes that cryptocurrencies are a speculative bubble that is bound to burst.

Here are some quotes from Warren Buffett about cryptocurrencies:

"I don't own any cryptocurrency, and I never will. I don't think they're a productive asset. They don't produce anything." (2018)

"If you told me you owned all the bitcoin in the world and you offered it to me for $25, I wouldn't take it because what would I do with it? I'd have to sell it back to you one way or another. It isn't going to do anything." (2020)

"Cryptocurrencies will come to a bad ending." (2018)

"I don't think Bitcoin is going to last." (2019)

"Cryptocurrencies are rat poison squared." (2019)

But at the same time, Michael J. Saylor, the founder of MicroStrategy, which is likely to own the most Bitcoins in the world, supports crypto heavily.

There are several reasons why Saylor is enthusiastic about crypto:

Store of Value: Saylor sees cryptocurrencies, especially Bitcoin, as a potential store of value. He believes that the limited supply of Bitcoin (only 21 million coins will ever exist) and its decentralized nature makes it an attractive alternative to traditional fiat currencies, which can be subject to inflation and central bank policies.

Digital Gold: Saylor often refers to Bitcoin as "digital gold". He sees it as a digital asset with many qualities traditionally associated with gold, such as scarcity, durability, and divisibility.

Long-Term Investment: Saylor has taken a long-term investment approach with Bitcoin. He sees it as a multi-decade investment opportunity and has stated that MicroStrategy's Bitcoin purchases are part of a strategy to protect the company's treasury assets from the potential devaluation of fiat currencies.

So, who's right?

I would suggest you only take their opinions as "information" to analyze for yourself.

Because the truth is, it's probably highly biased.

If you have a lot of Bitcoins instead of USD, this goes without saying that you would want Bitcoin to be highly valuable so that you'll not lose all of your assets.

If you have billions of USD and no Bitcoins, I'm sure you wouldn't like Bitcoins.

The fact is that the risk is there. This is why I don't encourage you to have more than 20% in this bucket.

Although you can push up to 30% depending on how well your other buckets are and your skill in acquiring income.

For this bucket, please make sure you clearly understand these remarks:

We're investing. Like investing in stocks, you're buying crypto to hold for the future as an asset for investment.

Only buy blue-chip cryptos for investment. As of releasing this book, the blue chips are Bitcoin and Ethereum. Bitcoin is the gold standard, while Ethereum is beyond a currency because it's a technology (a product) widely used in Web3 today.

But because they are high risk with the possibility of plummeting insanely, you should consider mitigating your risk. Don't invest ignorantly.

You see, due to the fact that they can plummet that way, it also means they can skyrocket like crazy.

And for that matter, there's a window of opportunity to reduce your risks even further.

This is the model that I'll use – selling to get cryptos at a discount.

I'm going to give you a theoretical illustration to teach what I mean. The numbers below are not real, just for demonstration:

Assuming I bought 1 ETH at $2,000.

If it goes up to $4,000 I'll sell 0.5 ETH of it to earn back my original investment and with that, I'm no longer having any risk, regardless of what's the price later on.

But I get to keep 0.5 ETH as my investment.

I would rather have less crypto in my portfolio with zero risk than worry I may lose money.

But to wait for it to reach $4,000 may not be so fast. Thus, even if it goes up to $3000 instead of $4000, I would consider getting back some of my investment. Maybe, I'll sell 0.5 ETH to earn back $1,500; with that done, I'll still have 0.5 ETH.

However, the 0.5 ETH in my portfolio would only cost me $500 bucks to own.

Although it's a theory, the craziest part is that it is possible that the ETH price can go up 2x.

You may need to monitor, but it doesn't need to be taking up your active time since the spike won't happen in a single day. There are apps that you can install into your smartphone, and when it hits a certain threshold you've set, it'll automatically alert you.

The goal here is always to minimize risk. The game of financial independence and debt-free is a marathon, and it's okay if you're earning less each time.

Because it's the accumulation of it that will lead you to your financial independence.

NEVER GET INTO TRADING.

Whether it's stock or crypto, please don't get into trading because trading is not investing.

I get it. It's easy to make money by trading.

When you make the money, you'll feel you can repeat this. You'll think that if you can make $100 daily, you can do this every day and make $3,000 monthly with minimal effort.

The reason why I know you'll think this way is because I've done that. And lost money.

In my opinion, if your goal is to make money, there are other ways that are less risky, such as starting an online business.

The entire book, MONEY: Present And Future, is to help you craft a life without money worries and, hopefully, to be debt-free.

Let me explain to you why trading can wipe you off entirely:

Remember what you've learned about Money Is Emotional?

You see, the market (regardless of stock or crypto) is inherently volatile, with prices fluctuating based on various factors such as economic conditions, company performance, geopolitical events, and investor sentiment. With sudden downturns or unexpected events can lead to significant losses.

Emotions can heavily influence trading decisions, leading to impulsive and irrational behavior.

Fear and panic during market downturns may prompt you to sell at a loss, locking in the losses and potentially missing out on future recoveries to build your portfolio.

One significant loss could take away ALL OF YOUR WINS.

Achieving financial freedom and debt-free typically requires a long-term perspective and a focus on wealth preservation and growth.

Trading in a speculative manner can undermine these goals.

By risking your income, you expose yourself to significant losses that may not be recoverable in time for other investments or to build up the portfolio.

Besides, let me ask you a frank question – have you ever met anyone who achieves financial freedom by trading?

I haven't, but I've met MANY with proper investments. Even if they don't achieve financial freedom, they're happy because they don't have to worry about losing.

Live Your Ambition and Spend What You Deserve

This chapter might resonate more after you've comprehended investing in the three buckets.

Why? Because I'm going to encourage you to spend your money as well.

I'm not extraordinarily wealthy, but as an average person, I've been able to live an extraordinary lifestyle because I've learned how to earn and spend effectively.

I've acquired a multi-million dollar weekend home, driven Porsche and Mercedes cars, and vacationed worldwide, visiting cities like Paris, Orlando, Las Vegas, London, Budapest, Amsterdam, Melbourne, Shanghai, Bangkok, Hong Kong, San Diego, Dubai, Rome, Santorini, Marseille, Shenzhen, Sydney, Mumbai, Prague, Jakarta, Los Angeles, Vancouver, and the list goes on.

While these expenditures might not yield financial returns, I don't regret any of them. Life isn't solely about money; I'm content in my 40s, knowing I've achieved all this. Hence, while it's crucial to save and invest, it's equally important to SPEND.

When you're young, ambitions and goals are a must.

Aim to own a beautiful house or a luxury car. Pursuing material rewards is not inherently evil.

I consistently tell my kids to have the drive to succeed and strive for life's finer things when they're young adults. There's no harm in aiming high, especially when there's nothing to lose.

In a professional setting in a job, the desire for money can motivate you to strive for promotions, take on challenging projects, and continuously improve your skills. It's not unusual for top performers in any industry to be driven, at least in part, by financial incentives.

Consider this: a promotion often comes with a pay raise. If you're motivated by increasing your earnings, you'll likely be more proactive in seeking opportunities to prove your worth, take on more responsibilities, and demonstrate leadership. This ambition can lead to career advancement and personal growth.

Regarding entrepreneurship, the desire for money can be an even more potent catalyst!

After all, one of the defining characteristics of entrepreneurs is their willingness to take risks in pursuit of financial rewards.

If you're driven to earn money, you might be more inclined to spot business opportunities, innovate, and bring new products or services to market. This drive can lead to job creation, economic growth, and societal improvements, besides the potential financial rewards for you as an entrepreneur.

Moreover, the desire for financial success can help you persevere through the inevitable challenges of entrepreneurship. Starting and running a business is hard work and often involves facing uncertainty, setbacks, and failures. If the potential for financial gain drives you, you'll be more likely to stick with it and work through the tough times, right?

No desire for money? Then you'll quickly give up your business when faced with great adversities.

Strangely, this chapter may seem contradictory to previous chapters, which advised against spending more than you earn and emphasized focusing on your three investment buckets.

If I were there in person, I could explain it better. However, here's my key message:

Being rich with no intent to spend the money is pointless. Of course, you might not be able to afford a luxury car next year with your current income, but there are other things you can happily afford.

My life principle has never been about accumulating a lot of money; rather, it's about having a good life with "more than enough" money to spend.

Living frugally could cost you friendships, experiences in your youth, and the chance to broaden your perspective by exploring new things in life.

The story of Ronald Read, a Vermont resident who led a modest life while amassing a significant fortune through wise and patient investing, illustrates this point. I wouldn't opt for such a lifestyle despite his frugality and considerable wealth. I would prefer to have reasonable vacations with my wife, drive a more excellent car, and so on if I could afford it.

Ultimately, the purpose of money is to be spent. It's a currency used to purchase something, and by itself, it does little until spent. The belief that spending money can bring happiness has a lengthy historical background, with many seeking material possessions and experiences to enhance their well-being and find happiness.

However, the relationship between money and happiness is complex. It's crucial to understand the limitations of material possessions, seek value-based spending, and ensure financial security and overall well-being.

The association between money and happiness can be traced back to ancient philosophical texts. Philosophers like Aristotle emphasized the pursuit of eudaimonia, which encompassed overall well-being and flourishing, including material prosperity.

Religious and spiritual traditions also addressed the relationship between wealth and happiness, often cautioning against excessive attachment to material possessions, such as in Buddhism.

In modern times, economic theories and consumer culture have reinforced the idea that spending money leads to happiness.

Therefore, use your wisdom to balance your life – spend to bring happiness, but don't overspend, and always keep your three investment buckets in mind.

The Hidden Money Traps

I refer to these as "hidden money traps".

Why?

Because, on the surface, it seems like you're winning or gaining an advantage. But there's a hidden string attached that isn't even visible. These traps will take your money away.

So, I urge you to be cautious.

Pay Later

The fintech industry has experienced explosive growth in recent years.

New technologies like artificial intelligence, blockchain, and cloud computing drive this growth. These innovations enable fintech companies to develop new financial products and services that are more efficient, secure, and convenient than traditional financial services.

Furthermore, the fintech industry's growth is propelled by increasing demand for financial services from consumers and businesses worldwide. Consumers seek more convenient and affordable ways to manage their finances, and businesses are exploring new methods to access capital and manage risk.

Consequently, the fintech industry is expected to continue expanding in the coming years. By 2030, the global fintech market is projected to reach $323 billion.

In this evolving landscape, a novel concept has emerged that encourages consumers to spend more, even without having the money to do so...

This brilliant concept is known as "Pay Later".

Many fintech companies now offer this option. For instance, a Pay Later* program allows you to pay for eligible purchases of $199 to $10,000 in monthly instalments. You choose the number of months (6, 12, or 24) you want to pay over, then make a fixed monthly payment.

* Subjected to change

To use Pay Later, you must create a PayPal account and link a credit or debit card. At checkout, if you're shopping with a participating merchant, you'll see Pay Later as a payment method. If you're eligible, you can select it and make your purchase.

PayPal performs a soft credit check to determine your eligibility. If you're approved, you can start making payments immediately. However, if you miss a payment, you'll be charged a late fee and may face a higher interest rate on future Pay Later purchases.

In Malaysia, there's GrabPay, which operates similarly to PayPal's Pay Later but provides you with a credit line.

From time to time, it'll send you promotions to buy stuff with the "good news" that you can afford to purchase items today because you can Pay Later.

Do I really need to elaborate further on how this is a hidden money trap?

Fintech companies with good track records often secure backing from investors or venture capitalists (VCs). There's a reason for this - these fintech companies stand to make a lot of money.

But how will they profit by giving you "free money" to spend?

Most people won't be able to pay back, and that's where the problems start.

This Pay Later scheme is even more dangerous than a credit card for luring you in…

They GIVE YOU MONEY TO SPEND. Many would be tempted to use that "free money" in their apps.

When you start spending, you don't feel the pain yet. You only feel the pleasure of buying the stuff you want. The more pleasure you get, the more you're going to spend.

Shopping Sales

Sounds strange for me to admit this, but shopping is a habit of mine.

In the past, whenever I visited a mall, I'd buy clothes, whether a T-shirt or a cap. I also liked to buy coats and jackets, which seemed strange since I didn't get to wear them because of the tropical weather here. We don't have autumn or winter.

Furthermore, because I work remotely and don't have any official meetings, the coats and suits are just for display. I don't get to wear them. Yet, I enjoyed buying them.

And oh, there's one more thing I liked to buy, which is redundant – sneakers and sports shoes. Compared to other guys, I have plenty.

So, why did I buy stuff I didn't need or couldn't use?

Because of two reasons: When I put them on, they looked great and were on sale.

It was hard to refuse such a deal. So the impulse to buy took over, and my brain justified it as a "worthwhile buy".

But the problem is, regardless of how worthwhile it is, if you can't use it or already have similar stuff, it's just an extra expense, and it clutters your life with MORE STUFF!

The illusion of saving can lead you to purchase clothes on sale, even if you don't truly need them. The perception of getting a good deal may override whether the item is a practical or essential purchase.

Over time, this can result in a wardrobe filled with unused or underutilized clothing, wasting money and resources.

Like me with my coats and suits. They're just collecting dust. You may convince yourself that you are financially responsible by buying clothes on sale, even if your overall spending exceeds your budget or financial goals. This can lead to misallocating funds and hinder progress toward long-term financial objectives.

And keep in mind that you're being influenced to buy as well. Apparel companies sometimes employ manipulative ways to create a sense of urgency or manipulate consumer desires. This can involve misleading claims, exaggerated discounts, or creating an artificial need for new clothing.

For example, consider a scenario where you enter a store to buy a specific item. You see a 'Buy 2, Get 1 Free' deal on a product that wasn't on your shopping list. It may seem like a great deal, but if you weren't planning to buy it, you're spending money that could have been saved or allocated elsewhere.

Clothing companies invest in advertising campaigns to create brand awareness and attract you. Eye-catching visuals, compelling storytelling, and aspirational messaging are often used to evoke desire and convince you of the value of their products.

So when you see the "on-sale" clothes subconsciously, you're already prepared to buy them because you're now getting a great deal.

And just like all of my advice, I don't put a statement saying, "Yes" or "No." Buy or don't buy. You'll need to be aware of what you're buying.

Here's the danger of shopping sales - it encourages impulse buying. You see something you like, and because it's "on sale," you buy it impulsively. But in reality, you don't really need it. You're just wasting your money.

It's important to understand that just because something is on sale doesn't mean it's a good deal.

Before you purchase, ask yourself - do I really need this? If the answer is no, then it's better to save money for something you need?

I'm still buying apparel regularly, just not on impulse anymore, and more importantly, I don't buy clothes I don't wear (like another jacket).

In this chapter, I'm choosing apparel and clothing as an example. But you must be aware of everything else you're spending "on sales". It could be smartphones, holiday packages, pens, coffee machines, luggage, etc.

Credit Cards: A Risky Cashflow Strategy

Are you tight with cash flow for your personal spending or business?

Don't worry. Just use the limit from the credit cards.

One of the favorite sales pitches used by marketers to sell their eCommerce or affiliate marketing training courses is this:

"You can start your business with $0 cost down. After researching products to sell and setting up your website, you only need to drive traffic to it using Facebook Advertising. And since you can use your credit card, you'll have 30 days to make your ad campaign profitable before paying for the ads."

In theory, it sounds beautiful.

But try implementing that in reality?

Of course, some will be talented and skillful enough to get it done successfully, but truth be told, most don't have that. Which means you're going to start owing the bank.

Just in case you're unaware of how much interest it will be and how deadly credit card debt can be, let me illustrate it to you…

Credit cards often carry high-interest rates, especially if the balance is not paid in full each month.

Credit cards usually charge a daily interest that compounds, meaning you pay interest on the initial amount you borrowed and the accumulating interest. This is why even a small credit card debt can balloon over time if you only make the minimum monthly payment.

The compounding effect of interest can make it challenging to eliminate debt quickly. Even a relatively small balance can quickly grow if only minimum payments are made, prolonging the time required to pay off the debt.

So, instead of leveraging compounding interest to earn, you're fighting against it by trying to pay it off. Credit card companies typically require a minimum monthly payment, usually a small percentage of the outstanding balance.

While paying the minimum may keep the account in good standing, it often only covers interest and fees, resulting in slow progress toward debt reduction. Individuals who consistently pay only the minimum may find themselves trapped in a cycle of long-term debt repayment.

You could be trapped in debt for years with just one wrong decision, wanting to manipulate the credit card system to get cash flow.

For instance, Caleb Hammer appeared on the Dave Ramsey show to share his story of how he accumulated $100,000 in credit card debt. It took him three years to pay off, but countless people could never find their ways to pay off anymore.

So, if you get into credit card debt, all your hard work is now spent fighting this financial crisis, which would eat up many of your years to grow.

This means none of your 3 buckets are filled up during this period. You are not set back a step; you're thrown off the court and need to find your way to get in again to play.

The longer it takes you to get into play again, the further you're going to be for achieving financial independence.

You can be slow, but never get yourself out of the court.

Money-Making Schemes

Almost anyone with money has fallen for money-making schemes before; it just depends on the sum.

I'm no different. I'm a human who has greed too. I've also paid for a money-making scheme; my friend referred it.

The only reason you have not heard from me about such is that I don't promote it to anyone. I've already known the money-making scheme is a form of a get-rich-quick scheme.

Money-making schemes are usually pyramid schemes.

This means that for the model to work, the "investors" (those folks who put their money into the scheme) will also act as the referrer, where they'll earn commissions for bringing more people into the scheme.

But wait. It continues because it's multi-levels of commissions. Thus, the referrer can build a "pyramid" of earnings from everyone below him.

Please keep in mind that this is different from any legit network marketing business. These money-making schemes require you not to do anything to earn! Yes, you'll still be guaranteed to make money even without referring anyone.

On top of that, it'll pay an absurdly high-interest rate compared to any conventional investment vehicle with a guarantee.

This is a good investment, isn't it?

Do nothing, guaranteed to earn and higher yield than anywhere else.

Yes…. Until the whole pyramid collapses and everyone panics.

Eventually, it'll collapse, and here are a few reasons:

Recruitment Dependency: Pyramid schemes depend on a constant influx of new participants to sustain the scheme (new participants are funding the commission of existing participants). As more people join the scheme, the recruitment pool diminishes, making it increasingly difficult to find new members. Eventually, the scheme reaches a point where recruitment slows down or stalls, which leads to its collapse.

Unsustainable Financial Structure: Pyramid schemes offer enticing financial rewards to early participants, often promising significant returns on their investments. However, these returns are typically funded by the investments of new recruits rather than actual profits generated through legitimate business activities. As new recruits decrease, the financial structure becomes unsustainable because those at the bottom of the pyramid, who joined later, are left with little or no opportunity to recover their investments.

Legal Intervention: Pyramid schemes are illegal due to their fraudulent nature. Law enforcement agencies will shut down these schemes. So, once authorities become aware of a pyramid scheme and launch an investigation, it becomes increasingly challenging for the scheme operators to continue their activities, leading to the "fly by night" operators.

In a pyramid scheme, there's no actual product. Participants are paying so that they'll get paid for doing nothing. Or they are recruiting to earn even more.

While there are several ways to identify a get-rich-quick scheme so you won't be scammed, these two are enough to tell the whole story…

Unrealistic Promises of High Returns: Be wary of any scheme that promises extraordinary profits or returns that seem too good to be true. Pyramid schemes often lure you with quick and substantial profits with minimal effort or risk. Remember, legitimate investments with high returns involve calculated risks and realistic expectations.

Lack of Tangible Products or Services: A legitimate business typically offers customers actual, tangible products or services with genuine value. If a company claims to have a business opportunity but lacks precise, concrete products or services, it's a warning sign. In a pyramid scheme, the focus is on recruiting others rather than selling products or services to customers. When they recruit, the pyramid company earns and gives some earnings to the recruiter.

Here's a metaphor to elaborate on how to identify a pyramid scheme and avoid getting scammed:

Imagine you're at a crowded marketplace, browsing through various stalls.

You come across a vendor who claims to have a magical money-making machine. He says that if you invest in his machine, you'll receive a never-ending stream of gold coins.

It sounds too good to be true.

In this scenario, the magical money-making machine represents the pyramid scheme. The vendor is the scheme's promoter, enticing you with promises of endless wealth. But let's break it down with our metaphor:

The Magical Machine: The machine represents the scheme's compensation structure. Instead of offering a legitimate product or service, the focus is solely on recruitment.

The device seems enticing, but there's no substance behind it.

Gold Coins: The gold coins represent the high returns promised by the scheme. Like the vendor's claims, these returns are shiny and captivating but not based on legitimate business activity. The coins are merely an illusion.

Crowded Marketplace: The crowded marketplace represents the world of investments and business opportunities. It's filled with legitimate businesses offering valuable products or services. But among them, some vendors are trying to sell you their magical machines. It's crucial to navigate through the crowd and identify genuine opportunities.

If you're thinking…

You can win the game by simply "getting out" before the pyramid bursts, I must disappoint you.

You're forgetting the X-factor again.

Money is emotional.

If you have a Magical Machine that churns out Gold Coins for you, can you sit still with just one Magical Machine to earn slowly?

Soon, you'll buy more Magical Machines and think your financial life is set.

Interestingly, this is not the worse yet. The worst is when you become greedy and start recruiting your friends to buy Magical Machines so that you can earn even more.

I have personally lost money to money-making schemes. It taught me a good lesson; this is why I can advise you so that you don't need to learn the hard way.

And keep in mind that quick-rich schemes are zero-sum games. If you're winning, someone else is losing. There's no such thing as both parties winning; someone has to lose for you to win.

To me, that's just bad karma. Bad money.

Investments Beyond Money: Nourishing Body, Mind, and Relationships

Now that you are well-versed with the Hidden Money Traps, what are NOT money traps?

Which ones are well worth spending on, even though there is no direct financial return as an investment?

Let's delve into the next part of this book…

Health: An Investment with Lifelong Returns

We've been talking a lot about financial stuff, haven't we?

While those are crucial topics, in this chapter, we're shifting gears to talk about an area that's even closer to the heart: health.

I was fortunate to have been educated about health early on in my life, during my entrepreneurship journey and when I was making considerable money.

This awareness arose from my involvement with a network marketing company that dealt with health and wellness products. The company taught me how to care for my health, and I started taking supplements.

Why is health so often neglected?

It's primarily because we're typically consumed with the pursuit of financial wealth, and sometimes, we only realize the importance of health when we're old!

The pursuit of economic prosperity is an inherent part of the human condition. However, amidst this relentless chase, we often lose sight of a more profound and subtler treasure: our health.

Your ability to work, innovate, contribute, and grow personally is fundamentally rooted in your health.

Imagine life as a beautiful, ornate ship.

Financial wealth may be the sails, the grand aspect everyone admires, propelling you forward with the wind. But health is your ship's hull, hidden beneath the surface, keeping you afloat and shielding you from the relentless ocean's waves. A ship can sail even with tattered sails, but a breached hull will send it to the ocean floor.

In the end, health is everything. It's your ship's hull, the foundation of your mansion, the cornerstone of your dream, happiness, productivity, and growth.

If there's one investment you should make in life, it should be your health because that is the most significant wealth.

Although this book is primarily about money, I urge you to use your money to keep yourself healthy. **This implies being willing to spend money on food that nourishes your body.**

Personally, I don't spend on gyms simply because my residence has a gymnasium.

The best health hack you can employ is to take supplements.

Supplements are like the supporting actors in our health story, adding a bit of flair when the lead character, our nutrition, falls short.

Now, on one hand, let's consider life without supplements.

Ideally, getting all your nutrients from a balanced diet would be best – fruits, veggies, lean proteins, whole grains, and whole shebang.

But let's be honest; not all of us have the luxury of an all-natural, perfectly balanced diet in our daily lives.

Our busy lives, work stress, or even access to fresh produce can make this ideal scenario hard to achieve.

This is where health supplements come in as effective solutions.

Sometimes, getting the amount of nutrients from our regular food is almost impossible.

For instance, I take resveratrol for its antioxidant benefits.

Resveratrol is a type of natural phenol and a phytoalexin produced by several plants, known for its potential antioxidant and anti-inflammatory properties. It's most commonly found in grapes.

While there is no official recommended daily allowance (RDA) for resveratrol from health organizations like the World Health Organization (WHO), some studies have used doses between 150 mg to 500 mg per day.

The resveratrol content in the skin of red grapes is typically in the range of 0.05-0.1 milligrams. This means that for me to get a minimum dose of resveratrol based on the research, I would need to eat about 1,500 red grapes per day.

This is why I say supplements are the health hack you can use unless you can eat over 1,000 grapes daily.

And then there are telomeres.

Telomeres are protective caps at the ends of your chromosomes. Every time a cell divides, the telomeres shorten a bit. When telomeres become too short, the cell can no longer divide and becomes inactive, "senescent," or dies. This process is often associated with aging, disease, and a higher risk of death.

So, what's the connection between telomeres and anti-aging?

The theory is that if telomere shortening is connected to aging, keeping our telomeres long should slow the aging process. The enzyme telomerase can add DNA sequence repeats to the telomere ends, effectively lengthening them.

Now, wouldn't it be great if you could slow down aging?

I want to have the energy and health to spend quality time with my kids as they grow up.

To protect and lengthen your telomeres, you can follow specific diets like focusing on whole foods, antioxidant-rich foods, foods rich in Omega-3 fatty acids, curcumin and quercetin-rich foods, and green tea.

Alternatively, I can use my money to invest in my health by buying supplements that contain these nutrients. It only takes me a few seconds to consume these capsules developed by top-notch doctors and scientists.

Of course, I'm not suggesting you take resveratrol or supplements for your telomeres, especially if you're young and not concerned about aging.

But the point is that your body needs some essential nutrients, and you should ensure that your money is "invested" in YOUR HEALTH.

You need health to go out there to earn money too.

Experiences: Priceless Treasures

When it comes to choosing between material possessions and experiences, people often have differing opinions.

A younger me might have agreed with a former girlfriend who believed that purchasing tangible goods, like a handbag, was a better investment than spending on travel.

Her reasoning was straightforward: a physical item, like a bag, lasts for years, whereas after a trip, you're left with nothing tangible.

When I was young, I agreed with her point.

As I've grown older, however, my perspective has drastically changed. Today, I would disagree with that viewpoint entirely.

When you travel, the experience you gain stays with you, not physically like a bag, but within your memory, for a lifetime.

Consider the tale of two friends, Jenny and Laura.

Jenny loved luxury—designer clothes, high-tech gadgets, and fast cars. For her 30th birthday, she decided to splurge on a new sports car costing $100,000.

Laura, conversely, treasured experiences more than possessions. An avid traveler and culture enthusiast, she chose to spend $10,000 on a month-long tour of Europe for her 30th birthday. She explored Rome, tasted wine in France, hiked the Swiss Alps, and immersed herself in Greece's history.

In the short term, Jenny's car seemed to be an enormous attraction. It was glossy, fast, and drew compliments. But with time, the novelty wore off, and the vehicle depreciated rapidly. Within a few years, it was worth only half of what she paid.

Laura's journey, however, enriched her life in a way that's hard to quantify. She returned home with unforgettable stories, newfound knowledge, and a broader perspective on life. Her memories were profoundly ingrained and continued to provide joy and inspiration.

Years later, both friends reflected on their 30th birthdays during challenging times.

Jenny's car, now old news and significantly devalued, offered little comfort. On the other hand, Laura's trip still brought her joy and motivation, reminding her of the world's beauty and resilience.

In essence, Laura possessed something money couldn't buy— rich, uplifting experiences that shaped her character and worldview.

A study from Cornell University in 2014 supports this concept. The study found that people derive more happiness from experiences than material goods. The joy from experiences increases over time as they become part of our identity, whereas satisfaction from material possessions diminishes.

This isn't to say that material possessions are worthless. However, for long-term happiness and 61ulfilment, investing in experiences like travel, events, or simply sharing a meal with loved ones can provide richer, longer-lasting satisfaction.

In our quest for financial freedom, we often forget to budget for experiences.

Consider setting aside a 'joy fund' each month or year, specifically for experiences. These experiences don't have to be extravagant but should foster learning, evoke joy, and create memories. These experiences could be the stepping stones to innovative ideas, opening up avenues for financial growth.

After all, can you really put a price on watching a sunset over a new city, tasting exotic cuisine, or forming bonds with new people?

Whenever I met people from India, I would talk with them and share that I've been to Mumbai and New Delhi. It makes them smile, knowing that people from other countries and races visit their country.

And I'll usually compliment them. I love the authentic vegetarian food there.

I couldn't say that if I've never visited Mumbai and tasted the food, right?

That experience has been with me for a lifetime, and I can connect with others from India.

These experiences, stored as beautiful memories, will accompany you throughout your life, long after physical goods have served their purpose.

While saving money and making sound investments for a secure future is essential, it's equally important to invest in living a fulfilled life with diverse experiences. Such an approach doesn't view money as an end in itself but as a means to enrich life.

The payoff? A life well-lived, filled with a treasure trove of memories, personal growth, and a heart full of contentment.

In the end, investing in experiences is not just about spending money; it's about choosing to live fully. And that, indeed, is truly priceless.

Skills: Endless Returns on Investment

Warren Buffett once said, "Whatever abilities you have can't be taken away from you. They can't be inflated away from you. The best investment by far is anything that develops yourself, and it's not taxed at all."

In other words, investing in learning new skills can be an exceptional decision, even if it isn't directly related to making money. The return on investment (ROI) can still be positive.

Let me illustrate this with a story from the life of Steve Jobs. In the late 70s, a young Steve Jobs attended Reed College in Oregon. He hadn't found his true passion yet, but his curiosity led him to take a calligraphy class.

This seemingly random decision to learn calligraphy had a profound impact on the future of Apple.

Jobs applied the lessons he learned in that class to the design of the Macintosh computer, making it a product that was not only functional but also elegant and beautiful. The calligraphy class shaped Jobs' understanding of design aesthetics and attention to detail, which later became Apple's defining traits.

Let me tell you a story about my daughter and her incredible love for art.

Her name is Marireis, and from the moment she could draw, it was evident that art held a special place in her heart.

As her parents, we wholeheartedly encouraged her artistic pursuits, never imagining the possible entrepreneurial path ahead.

Our goal was simple: to nurture her passion and watch her creativity bloom.

And there's no intention of making money with the skill.

We saw art as a way for her to express herself and find joy rather than a means of financial gain. We wanted her to explore her imagination freely without the pressure of commercializing her talent. Little did we know that fate had something extraordinary in store for her while she was still schooling in elementary school.

Because opportunity arises with digital art, which is NFT.

NFTs allow artists to transform their creations into unique digital assets and sell them using blockchain technology. It was a chance for Marireis to share her art with a global audience while staying true to her creative spirit.

So, I converted her art into NFTs and sold it successfully online.

I've carefully digitized each piece, ensuring that the essence and beauty of her art remained intact without tempering its originality. With the power of the internet and social media, we showcased her work to art enthusiasts and collectors worldwide. To our amazement, Marireis' NFTs sold successfully, finding appreciative owners who valued her unique talent.

We'll launch her following NFT collection, the Marireis Elementary, her work for the past three years when she was still in elementary school.

And depending on when you're reading this chapter, it may already be out in the world, enchanting art lovers and collectors with heartfelt expressions.

What started as a simple love for art has taken my daughter on an incredible journey.

The world of NFTs has given her an unexpected platform to showcase her talent and connect with people who appreciate her unique perspective.

So, imagine this:

You decide to invest cash in learning a new skill, like coding.

You start taking online courses, joining coding boot camps, and getting your hands on projects. Fast forward a bit, and guess what?

You've become a coding expert!

You can even freelance on the side and make some serious income. That's what I call a return on investment.

But wait, there's more. Let's talk about your personal growth.

When you learn a new skill, it's like unlocking a hidden superpower within yourself. It's an opportunity to expand your horizons and challenge yourself in ways you never thought possible.

For example, let's say you've always been interested in photography. you decide to invest in a camera and take a photography course.

As you develop your skills, you start capturing breath-taking images and expressing your unique perspective. Not only does it bring you joy and fulfilment, but it also boosts your confidence and unleashes your creative potential.

So, my advice is this: don't try to save money by investing in yourself and learning new skills.

It's like planting seeds of opportunity that can grow into something extraordinary. Whether it's coding, photography, cooking, or playing a musical instrument, the possibilities are endless.

Take that leap, and watch yourself transformed. Trust me; you won't regret it.

Family: Spending That Enriches Your Life

The last piece of "Not Money Traps" is giving.

So, you're a bit short this month to contribute to your 3 buckets because you took your parents out for a holiday.

To me, this is not an expense. Yes, it's considered an expense in a conventional cash flow ledger, but it's more a deposit towards love.

If your parents are still with you and you're being frugal with them, you should remember how much they've spent for you.

Their currency is love. They spent for you because of love.

If you can convert money into expressing love and you're not doing it, why would you want to earn money?

Because with or without realizing it, one of the purposes of having money is to gain affection.

Although I cannot put a blanket truth that the affection from family is authentic, it should be that way.

I can only speak from personal experience, but my mum loves me regardless of whether I spend money on her. That said, I know it makes her happy when I do, which brings me joy.

Let's delve into why spending money on your family is a worthwhile investment:

Investment in Memories: You purchase memories when you spend on your family. Those family trips or game nights become cherished moments that last a lifetime. Like when I took my kids to watch Cirque Du Soleil – they were utterly captivated. You can't attach a price tag to experiences like that.

Fostering Relationships: Often, it's not about grand gestures but the small, thoughtful things. Treating your parents to dinner, getting your sibling that book they've been talking about, or buying your kid that game they've been eyeing. These small actions can strengthen relationships and show your family you care.

The Joy of Giving: Spending on your family also brings you happiness. Seeing their faces light up when you surprise them with a gift or a trip is priceless. It's an investment in their joy and, by extension, yours.

Support and Empowerment: Sometimes, spending money on family is about enabling them to pursue their dreams. Maybe your sibling wants to start a business, and you decide to invest in it, or your daughter loves baking and you buy her baking supplies. You're nurturing their ambitions, which can lead to personal growth and development.

Building Traditions: Money spent on traditions or celebrating milestones is always well-spent. You could have a yearly family holiday or never miss a Marvel movie in the cinema. These traditions become part of your family's identity and shared memories, creating a sense of unity.

Gratitude and Reciprocation: Finally, spending on family can be a way of expressing gratitude and giving back. Your parents likely invested a lot in raising you. Spending on them in their old age can be a way of saying thank you and reciprocating their love and care.

We often view money as numbers in a bank account. But it's more than that. It's a tool that can do a world of good when used wisely.

One of the best ways to use that tool? Thoughtfully spending on your family and loved ones.

Please note that I'm not suggesting you splurge on designer items or buy everyone the latest smartphone. I'm talking about meaningful generosity. It's about expressing love and care through words, actions, and choices.

These gestures of generosity do more than make someone smile. They strengthen bonds and foster gratitude and abundance in your family. They send a clear message to your loved ones: you value them, and you're there to support them.

In return, you'll be rewarded with love, respect, and unity.

Money comes and goes, but the memories, bonds, and love you foster are priceless.

The Random Money Advice

Welcome to the "Random Money Advice" chapter.

This is where I will share three pieces of advice about money that I've found incredibly useful. Now, when I say "random," I mean it. These nuggets of wisdom aren't about any specific aspect of money management. They could be lessons I've learned from my mistakes or thoughts on how I use money in my day-to-day life.

These insights aren't just motivational quotes to hang on your wall; they're practical and applicable. They can help you avoid financial pitfalls I've stumbled into, or they might even steer you towards opportunities that could make you a fortune. Who knows?

One more thing - I'm always coming up with new pieces of advice. So, I've set up a newsletter to share these insights. Make sure to sign up for it at moneypresentandfuture.com.

If you have your phone with you, here's the QR code:

So, ready to dive in? Let's explore these three pieces of random money advice together.

Learning from Kiyosaki and Ramsey:
A Word of Caution

I appreciate Robert Kiyosaki and Dave Ramsey. I really do.

I got my first real education about money from Kiyosaki. If you haven't picked up his classics, like 'Rich Dad Poor Dad' or 'Cashflow Quadrant,' you're missing out. They're great for sparking motivation and raising awareness about financial freedom.

But remember, not all advice suits all situations.

For instance, Kiyosaki wasn't a crypto fan initially, but now he seems to be advocating it. It's not about right or wrong; it's about perspectives. And let's face it, we all make mistakes.

It could also depend on his financial situation or what's currently trending in the market.

Kiyosaki loves 'good debts' because they create cash flow without interest. Sounds great, but does he show how he's winning with his debts? That's something to ponder.

Does he disclose his debts to validate this strategy's financial success? If he does, I stand corrected and would appreciate it if you could point me to that resource to learn together.

The thing is, theory and reality can be vastly different.

Let's talk about Dave Ramsey.

He's done wonders in helping people eliminate debt. His advice on saving and avoiding lavish spending is valuable.

But is thrifting and savings the only path to wealth? I think there's a more enjoyable way to freedom.

Life is abundant, and money helps us experience it. So, if we're thrifty during our youth, even with extra money later, can it buy back time and experience?

For me, youth is the 40s because my 20s have passed. I'd rather spend money considerately now than have an enormous pile of money in my 60s. By then, I'd have lost 20 years of youth, and there will be things I won't be able to enjoy anymore.

Suppose I'm an adventurous person, and my goal is to climb Mount Kilimanjaro. Sure, I could still do it in my 60s, but I'd enjoy it more in my 40s. Spending money on training and expeditions means I'll save less. But with the right plan and strategy, I'll still be well-off in my 60s, just less. And that's okay. I want to live fully, be happy, and contribute back.

Sometimes, a picture says a thousand words, right?

I use one of TikTok's filters to show how I look like when I'm old:

The young folks taught me this: YOLO. You only live once.

So, what if you could earn to replace the income you're spending?

Because earning extra income is relatively easy.

The Coffee Paradox: Understanding the True Value of Small Expenses

I go to a café every day to enjoy a coffee.

And yes, I'm fully aware of the financial advice floating around, telling me I'm throwing away potential investments with every cup.

I honestly don't know how much a cup of latte will cost you in your country because it is different if you're in San Diego vs. Penang. But let's assume it's $5 for a simple discussion here.

Now, you might think, "Is it worth skipping out on a small pleasure in life just to save $5?"

Before we dive into this controversial topic, I need you to understand the broader context of saving that $5 versus continuing to enjoy your daily coffee. Have you ever heard of the butterfly effect?

Imagine chilling at a park and seeing a cute little butterfly flapping its wings. You might think, "Aw, that's nice," and not think much of it. But here's the kicker: that tiny flutter from the butterfly stirs the air around it, which stirs up a bit more air, and even more air, and before you know it, it's caused a whole ripple effect.

That might sound far-fetched, but let's follow this phenomenon further.

These little changes in the air could eventually build up into more significant changes. Picture a butterfly flapping its wings in Brazil and causing a tornado in Texas.

The idea here is that even small actions can have big, unexpected effects down the line, especially in complex systems like the weather. That's the butterfly effect in a nutshell—it's all about how little things can end up making a big difference.

Now, you might ask, "What does my daily coffee have to do with butterflies?" Let's delve a little deeper…

Consider if you chose to forego that daily $5 coffee.

You might reason, "It's just $5; how much of a difference could it make?" But remember the butterfly. The small action of saving that $5 daily, like the butterfly flapping its wings, can cause a ripple effect over time.

Say you invest that $5 every day. Over a year, you'd have saved $1,825. Let's say you decide to invest this amount annually over 30 years, with a modest return of 5%. By the end of these 30 years, your coffee money would have grown to approximately $125,000. Not bad for a small daily saving, right?

More importantly, it's not just about the money you've accumulated; it's about the shift in your mindset. This little thrift act could fundamentally change how you view and handle money. Choosing to save, and forgoing instant gratification for future rewards, signals a shift from a consumption mindset to an investment mindset. It's about realizing that small sacrifices today can lead to significant gains in the future.

Now that you understand the context, here's the thing - this isn't to say that you should deprive yourself of all life's pleasures.

If you truly love that morning coffee ritual, it's perfectly okay.

The goal isn't to make yourself miserable by cutting all expenses; it's to be mindful of where your money is going and ensure it aligns with your values and goals.

With that context in place, I would rather continue to have my coffee and find ways to earn the $5 with different means instead of saving for it. Because when you are forcing yourself to give up little joys and pleasures you can afford in life, in my opinion, you're damaging your wealth mindset without realizing it.

Think about it.

Telling yourself that you're not worth it, that you cannot even afford a cup of coffee, that you need to live frugally in this world... these thoughts can negatively impact your wealth mindset.

And a damaged wealth mindset can affect your financial decisions in the future and even your happiness.

When people are overly thrifty, they may develop what's often called a scarcity mindset. Sendhil Mullainathan and Eldar Shafir, in their book "Scarcity: Why Having Too Little Means So Much," suggests that when we feel we don't have enough of something (in this case, money), we can become hyper-focused on that perceived lack. This narrow focus can make it harder for people to see opportunities and make long-term plans crucial to building wealth.

Moreover, a 2007 paper by Guiso and Paiella from the Bank of Italy showed that risk aversion negatively correlates with wealth, suggesting that overly thrifty individuals who avoid financial risk may also prevent the opportunity to accumulate wealth.

But here's the good news, what if you can EARN to replace the "loss" income you're using to spend?

I'll cover some ideas and ways in other chapters because it's not very hard to earn some extra income.

In my case, it also justifies tremendously to spend on my coffee because the café's environment is conducive for me to work. With that, it allows for higher productivity and better-quality output work. All for just $5. This means the 30 days x $5 = $150 expense is giving me a higher ROI as my work will generate much more than $150 of expense. So, sometimes, your expense is not an expense. It's just intangible to be seen as a positive ROI.

While this chapter focused on coffee, the underlying message applies to any minor, daily expense.

It's not about completely eliminating these expenses but understanding the value they bring to your life.

If your daily latte brings you joy, fuels your productivity, or even provides a quiet moment on a busy day, then that $5 may be well spent. It's about being mindful of our spending, recognizing the intrinsic value, and weighing it against the cost.

So, the next time you reach for your wallet, pause for a moment and consider the actual value of that expense.

If it enhances your life in a meaningful way, then by all means, enjoy it without guilt. Remember, money is a tool to enhance your life, not a chain that restricts it— every decision you make and every dollar you spend contributes to your personal journey of financial wisdom.

You're the one in control.

If It's An Ad, Stay Away

Picture this: a humble baker named Ben lives in a town named Fortune.

While Ben kneads dough one sunny afternoon, a stranger strolls into his bakery shop. With a cryptic smile, the stranger spins a tale of a lucrative investment opportunity - a gold mine, untouched and brimming with wealth, waiting for an investor.

Intrigued, Ben listens. The prospect of turning his hard-earned savings into a fortune is tempting. But amidst the allure of the golden dream, a simple yet significant question pops into Ben's mind: "Why me?"

"Why share this golden opportunity with a stranger?" Ben asks, his eyes narrowing. "If this mine is as rich as you claim, wouldn't you offer it to your loved ones or friends before strangers?"

The stranger shrugs, the cryptic smile never leaving his face. "Well, Ben, there's a finder's fee. If you invest, I gain too."

At that moment, Ben understands. The stranger isn't presenting this opportunity out of kindness or because he thinks Ben deserves a break. The stranger stands to gain from Ben's investment.

Thanking the stranger for his time, Ben declines the offer. Sure, the thought of easy wealth is enticing, but Ben realizes that when a stranger offers you an opportunity too good to be true, there's often more to the story.

After all, if it was such a good deal, why would the stranger not offer it to his family or friends first?

So, Ben returns to kneading his dough, a little wiser. His bakery might not be a gold mine, but it's a wealth source of its own.

In the investment world, keeping our eyes open, our minds sharp, and our hearts guarded is crucial. There's wisdom in recognizing that the best opportunities often come from diligent research, keen understanding, and sometimes, from listening to our instincts, just like our humble baker, Ben.

Aren't ads "strangers"?

Today's ads are not in newspapers but on Facebook, Google, YouTube, etc. They offer investment opportunities in startups, real estate, cryptos, etc.

You might ask a straightforward question:

If these investments yield money so easily, why should they advertise it?

By right, they would be "sold out" on their own and, perhaps, even have a waiting list.

Usually, when the opportunity is "open to the public," it often means it's no longer a hot opportunity — for example, real estate investment opportunities.

When you see promoters promoting real estate properties for sale in the mall, all the good units likely have already been taken, and these are the "leftovers" that were not sold out.

But this isn't to say all opportunities from ads are bad. There could be a reason why the investment opportunity still needs to advertise.

From my experience, hidden investment opportunities are only uncovered in two ways:

1. Contacts And Network

Networking can often expose you to genuinely valuable investment opportunities. Building a network of knowledgeable, trustworthy individuals is like building a lighthouse amid a busy marketplace. This network, composed of mentors, peers, and professionals knowledgeable about money, will shine a light on those hidden opportunities and help you make wise decisions.

Start by reaching out to those within your circles - friends, family, colleagues, or mentors. Share your interests and your intent to invest. Opportunities often come from casual conversations. Attend seminars, join financial forums, and participate in local community events - the more people you meet, the more comprehensive your network becomes, and the greater your exposure to potential opportunities.

Remember, networking isn't just about taking; it's about giving too. Share knowledge, lend a helping hand, and foster genuine relationships. This goodwill strengthens your reputation and often circles back to you through opportunities.

2. Due-Diligent Research

Hidden financial opportunities need to be found, not given. They're like the rarest pearls - they're not found lying on the beach; you have to dive deep into the ocean, often braving the unknown to unearth them. That's where diligent research comes in.

Diligent research involves immersing yourself in understanding the opportunity from various angles - the practicality, the potential, the risk, and so on. It's about going beyond the surface-level news or advice from acquaintances and genuinely understanding the potential of an investment opportunity.

This is not a "how to" investment book, but we could learn from investors about the lesson of due diligence.

Take Peter Lynch's investment strategy as an example. Lynch successfully managed the Fidelity Magellan Fund from 1977 to 1990 but didn't make his fortune by following hot tips or jumping on bandwagons. He made it by doing his homework. He spent countless hours researching companies, visiting their offices, and talking to their executives to get a clear picture of their operations.

Lynch was a firm believer in "investing in what you know." He looked for companies that he understood and saw daily around him. This led him to invest heavily in consumer and retail companies, leading to some of his biggest successes.

For instance, Lynch famously invested in Taco Bell, Dunkin' Donuts, and The Limited - all companies he encountered and understood in his everyday life. Under his management, the Fidelity Magellan Fund averaged an annual return of 29.2%, making it the best-performing mutual fund in the world.

So, what can we learn from Lynch's strategy to uncover hidden opportunities?

That the path to finding hidden investment opportunities is paved with knowledge, patience, and diligence, it's about understanding that these opportunities won't just fall into your lap - you need to go out and find them. You must dive into that ocean, delve into the nitty-gritty of financial statements and market trends, and find your pearls.

And it's not about getting lucky by stumbling upon an opportunity on Facebook.

How I Lost My Bitcoins

I've been through the painful experience of losing all my cryptocurrencies, not once but twice.

Let's take a trip down memory lane and discuss the first time I lost all my bitcoins. It wasn't because I forgot my key phrase; no, I'm much too careful about that. I lost my digital wealth because I wasn't watching my money closely enough.

In the heyday of bitcoins, ICOs or Initial Coin Offerings became a hot topic. To understand what ICOs are, let's first understand IPOs (Initial Public Offerings). An IPO is a process where a private company offers its shares to the public for the first time, with the aim of raising capital for growth and expansion. Famous companies like Facebook and Amazon underwent this process before their shares were listed on the stock exchanges.

On the other hand, an ICO is similar to an IPO but involves the sale of digital tokens or coins rather than shares. These tokens are built on blockchain technology, the backbone of cryptocurrencies like Bitcoin. ICOs are often used by startups to circumvent the stringent and regulated process of capital raising from venture capitalists or banks.

The allure was strong. During the peak of the ICO boom, it wasn't unusual to see a tenfold return on your investment, or more if you were lucky.

A friend of mine who was enjoying considerable success with ICOs offered to handle my investments for me. Greed got the better of me, and I transferred all my bitcoins to him for trading.

Luck, however, wasn't on my side. The ICO market crashed, locking all my bitcoins into ICO tokens that were now worthless. I had given my friend complete control over my bitcoins, so I lost everything.

The lesson here isn't just about greed.

The bigger takeaway is to never relinquish control of your money, especially to someone else. In other words, always be the one who watches your money grow.

Here's why: First, I didn't understand how ICOs worked.

Second, I had no idea how my friend was trading. I gambled on two fronts - trusting my friend entirely and betting on the volatile ICO market.

The rule of thumb is always to have control over your own money. Many celebrities have gone broke because they trusted someone else to manage their finances.

Today, I decide where to invest my money. I'm not an investment guru and don't spend hours analyzing company balance sheets. I invest based on my understanding and knowledge. For example, I don't put my money into mutual funds.

With mutual funds, you're handing over your money to fund managers to invest on your behalf. Whether the fund thrives or not, I think it doesn't affect the fund manager financially. They make their money from management charges for buying or selling mutual funds. It doesn't sound like a mutually beneficial arrangement to me.

However, in reality, there will be times when you need an expert to help your money grow too.

This could be due to a need for more skills or time. When that happens, my criteria are simple. The expert must be in the same boat as me, meaning if I lose, they lose too. Also, I must retain total control over my money.

Consider my ICO experience. Although my friend was in the same boat as me (he lost money too), we didn't set a parameter, like deciding not to invest all the bitcoins. If we had done that, even with the loss, we would still be in a good financial position today, considering the current Bitcoin price.

The crux of the matter is, if someone else manages your money, ensure you mitigate as many risks as possible. Don't be lured by the promise of quick riches.

In the cryptocurrency world, there's a method called 'staking,' where you can earn crypto by locking up your existing coins.

This is similar to earning interest from a savings account. However, if you're willing to take the time to learn, you could have more control by staking on self-custody with Rocket Pool or Lido, even though it might yield less. This way, you can remove the risk of losing your cryptos by not relinquishing control to the crypto exchange.

The easier route may not always be the safer one. The key to securing your wealth lies in vigilance, control, and understanding the risks involved. After all, you're the best guardian of your wealth.

Shaping Your Future Wealth

Ever heard of the saying, "You must learn to walk before you can run?"

Well, the same holds true for financial freedom. We have to secure our present before we can build a prosperous future.

That's precisely what we've been doing in the first part of this book - understanding how to spend wisely, put our money to work, and grow it through investments.

Now, here's the secret sauce: Your future is sculpted by the decisions you make and the actions you take TODAY.

That's why so many people find themselves in a financial rut - drowning in debt, living paycheck to paycheck, or lacking any form of passive income. They are busy trying to douse the financial fire burning in their present. I would've been in the same boat if I hadn't learned these vital lessons early on.

The truth is, these financial fires shouldn't have ignited in the first place.

But if they did, the goal should be to extinguish them in the present to secure a financially free future, not just to get immediate relief.

That's why setting the right expectations is crucial.

Falling into deeper financial holes due to desperation or rash decisions won't help anyone.

So, the good news? You've got this!

Manage your expectations realistically.

Don't get lured by flashy "Become a Millionaire Overnight" promises when you haven't solidified your three financial buckets yet.

"MONEY: Present and Future" isn't about hyping you with dreams of instant riches. It's about making you aware of the potential and pitfalls of money and how you can navigate towards financial independence.

This book is your practical playbook.

The goal is simple: Follow the playbook, and years from now, you'll be debt-free and financially secure, with money to spend each month.

I wrote this book for my kids, so they have many years to apply. If you don't have that many years in comparison, then you may need to work harder. It's doable.

So, to secure a prosperous future, you must learn how to expand your other two buckets:

Bucket #2: Low-Risk Investments That Are Safe In The Long Run

Bucket #3: High-Risk Investments With High Returns

Hence, you'll need to learn how to earn faster than your current income. But remember, while you're doing this, if you're under any employment with a company, ensure you're not violating your company's policies.

In today's age, with so much abundance, your company should be supportive if your side gig doesn't interfere with your primary job responsibilities.

As this book doesn't delve into employment intricacies, I'll leave it at that.

Just ensure you're treading on the right path.

Smart Side Hustles: How to Choose Wisely

You've probably heard of the term 'side hustle', right?

If you're like most people, you probably have.

But what's the big deal about it? And how is it different from starting your own business? Let's dissect this and see what's what.

Think about your full-time job as your main stage performance - it's grand, necessary, and pays the bills. Your side hustle, however, is like your rehearsal sessions, where you fine-tune your skills, explore new roles, and add extra income to your pocket. But here's the twist - sometimes, these practice sessions can lead to a blockbuster solo performance.

The primary difference between a side hustle and a business lies in how you earn money.

A side hustle often means you swap your time for money.

Given that there are only so many hours in a day, this can limit how much you earn. On the other hand, a business is like a well-oiled machine that keeps churning out money, often without you having to put in an equal amount of time.

This is not necessarily passive income but rather leverage income - using a small amount of time to yield large financial output.

At the same time, I will teach you something different here - Your side hustle isn't meant to be your primary source of income. Your regular job should cover your everyday expenses. Rather, it's an opportunity to speed up filling your three financial buckets, particularly if your first bucket isn't full yet.

So what makes for a good side hustle?

Well, consider it as a stepping stone or a launchpad that can catapult you toward your ultimate goal of running a business.

Ideally, this business should be online because an online business offers several distinct advantages:

Scalability: An online business can grow rapidly and reach a global audience relatively easily.

Low Operating Cost: Unlike traditional businesses, online businesses don't require a physical storefront, significantly reducing overhead costs.

Minimal Resources: Starting an online business doesn't require a massive investment or a large team. Often, all you need is a good internet connection, a computer, and your unique skills or products.

Freedom to Manage: An online business allows you to work from anywhere, anytime. You're not tied down by traditional office hours or locations.

Now, what should your side hustle be that still aligns with becoming an online entrepreneur or marketer one day?

Here are two solid options to consider when you want to start a side hustle:

Freelance in the Gig Economy

The beauty of the gig economy is that it allows you to monetize your existing skills. You earn by doing what you're already good at. If you're a talented writer, take on freelance writing projects. If graphic design is your thing, offer your services on platforms like Fiverr or Upwork.

Let's dive into more examples to make this crystal clear.

Imagine you're dreaming of one day running your own online consulting service. A great side hustle for you would be to get a part-time job or gig at a consulting firm. This could be as a junior consultant, assistant, or even in an administrative role!

Step 1: Pinpoint Your Interest

First things first, identify your passion and skills. Are you a numbers whiz or a problem-solving person? Write down your skills and strengths - this is no time to be modest. Along with your abilities, think about what really sparks your interest. After all, your side hustle should be something you genuinely enjoy.

Now, it's time for some research. Look into various types of consulting gigs that align with your skills and interests. Browse online forums or even reach out to people already in the field. They can offer valuable insights into what the job entails.

Step 2: Seek Opportunities

Now, let's turn your attention to finding gigs that align with your skills and goals. Craft an impressive profile that highlights your strengths and experiences. If you have, be sure to include real-life instances where you've applied these skills.

You can use platforms like LinkedIn, Upwork, or Fiverr to showcase your profile and seek opportunities. Also, tap into your network, let your connections know that you're open to part-time consulting gigs. You'd be surprised how many opportunities can come from word-of-mouth.

Step 3: Absorb & Learn

Be a go-getter: Don't sit around waiting for tasks. Show them you're proactive and ready to contribute.

Be curious: If you're puzzled about something, ask. People love to share what they know.

Be open: Feedback is your friend. It'll help you grow and become even more awesome at what you do.

Be observant: Watch how the experts are doing it. There's a wealth of knowledge there.

Be friendly: Make friends and build relationships – even online. These folks might be your future business contacts.

Side Hustle With Multi-Level Marketing (MLM)

I know MLMs can be controversial, but hear me out. They offer a platform to develop essential skills for free (or at minimal cost) that can be valuable in your journey. Here's what you stand to gain:

i. Personal Growth: MLMs push you out of your comfort zone and teach you valuable lessons about resilience, perseverance, and motivation.

ii. Sales Skills: You'll learn how to sell, a crucial skill in any business or entrepreneurial venture.

iii. Income Potential: While you shouldn't expect to get rich overnight, MLMs can offer additional income.

iv. Networking: You'll meet and work with a diverse group of people, expanding your network, which can be beneficial down the line.

v. Leadership Lessons: You can learn effective leadership strategies and techniques by observing your upline leaders.

vi. Free Training: Most MLM companies provide free training and resources to help you succeed because the more you succeed, the more they succeed financially.

vii. Industry Insight: MLMs offer a unique learning opportunity about a specific industry. For example, when I joined a wellness-focused MLM in the past, I gained insights about health and wellness that have been beneficial in my personal life today.

So the first step to starting an online business is to start a side hustle.

I'll walk you through how to get started with this after I've covered about starting and building an online business.

This is just going to get more exciting...

Part-Time Pursuit: Your Online Business Blueprint

If I'm honest, this chapter presented a unique writing challenge.

Here's why: The digital landscape shifts quickly and unpredictably. Let's imagine a scenario where I provide detailed instructions on advertising your business on Facebook. But then, Facebook decided to overhaul its advertising system the next day. Suddenly, my advice is obsolete and, at worst, potentially misleading.

That's not what we want.

So, instead of offering you precise steps tied to specific platforms that might change overnight, I'll aim to equip you with overarching principles. The aim here is to provide you with strategies that are adaptable and resilient to change – just like a good business should be.

Starting and growing an online business has many variables. Consequently, it's impossible to encapsulate everything in a single chapter.

But don't worry; there's plenty of help out there. You can find tutorials on Google and YouTube or even use AI to get answers to your questions. There are also many courses that can guide you in building your online business.

Just be sure to do your homework – carefully review and assess the credibility of any course before investing your time and resources into it.

There are five main types of online businesses that I will introduce to you.

I'll give you a single model for each type to illustrate the concept. This should help you grasp the big picture and hopefully kindle the spark of an idea that you can fan into a flame.

Idea #1: E-commerce - Your Launchpad for Selling Physical Products

So, let's get rolling with the first idea on our list - selling physical products through e-commerce. I know it might sound a bit intense at first, but believe me, once you get the hang of it, it's like learning to ride a bicycle.

Step 1: Scouting for the Right Product

First, we need to find a product we can sell. Think of something that piques your interest and that you believe has potential. Hop onto Amazon, or if you're in Asia like me, you could check out Shopee or Lazada. Basically, any popular online marketplace where you are. Treat this like a treasure hunt; you're searching for that golden product.

Step 2: Test the Waters with Affiliate Marketing

Found a product? Awesome. Now, before we jump in, we need to test the waters. We're going to promote the product as an affiliate. This means that you earn a bit of commission for every sale that happens through your promotion. It's like a sneak peek into the product's potential. If it's selling like hotcakes, we're onto something.

Step 3: Private Label Your Product

Once you've tested the waters and found that the product sells, it's time to make it your own. This is where private labeling comes in. You're going to source the product and sell it under your own brand. By doing this, you're not just selling a product but building a brand. This gives you greater control over pricing, marketing, and customer experience.

Step 4: Find Your Sweet Spot - The Niche Market

Next, we need to find our sweet spot. This is a niche market where we can introduce more products. A niche market is like our own little corner in the vast online marketplace. It's smaller, specialized, and the best part - less crowded. We're going to make this corner ours and fill it with products that people want.

Step 5: Boost Your Shopping Cart Value

The goal is to get our customers to buy more in a single transaction. It's like selling a whole outfit instead of just a shirt, increasing our 'shopping cart value'. The more they spend in one go, the more we earn, and the better we can cover our advertising costs.

Starting an e-commerce side hustle might seem like a big task, but it's just a series of small steps. Start by finding a product, testing it out, making it your own, finding your niche, and working on boosting your shopping cart value.

Idea #2: Selling Services - Unleashing Your Expertise

Okay, let's dive into the second idea - selling services. Now, I know what you're thinking: "But I'm not an expert at anything!" Well, you might be surprised. We all have unique skills and experiences; trust me, someone out there could benefit from what you know or can do.

Option 1: Coaching - Share Your Wisdom

If you've got expertise or knowledge in a specific field, why not consider coaching? Whether it's fitness, finance, business, or cooking, there are people willing to pay for your guidance. And the best part? You get to help others grow while making some extra cash. It's like teaching a dance class - you're sharing the steps you've mastered so others can enjoy the dance too.

You'd be surprised how many people are willing to pay for your wisdom and guidance!

Option 2: Done-For-You Services

Not into coaching? No worries. Another avenue you can explore is offering done-for-you services. For instance, you could set up and manage e-commerce stores, create captivating content for social media, or even design stunning websites. This could be a great option if you've got the skills and enjoy the work.

It's like being a backstage crew member in a theatre - you handle the technical stuff, and the show goes smoothly.

Marketing Your Services:

Now, here comes the fun part - getting your services out there. How do we do this? Well, it's like throwing a party - you've got to send out the invites...

1. Your Own Social Media - The Launchpad

First, start with your social media. Let your network know what you're up to and how you can help them. It's like telling your friends about your new venture and asking them to spread the word.

2. Free Service - The Hook

Next, consider offering your services for free in exchange for testimonials and referrals. This is a great way to build your portfolio and establish credibility. It's like asking your happy customers to vouch for your awesome service. Plus, it gives you some hands-on experience.

3. Free Trials - The Teaser

Lastly, try offering free trials to potential clients. It's a no-risk way for them to test out your service. If they like it, they'll probably want more.

You don't need a fancy degree or years of experience. Just take what you're good at, package it as a service, and get it out there.

Idea #3: Bridging Offline Businesses to the Online World

Let's talk about another exciting idea for your online venture - bridging offline businesses to the online world. This is all about taking products or services traditionally sold in a physical location and bringing them to the online market.

Examples of Offline Businesses to Bring Online:

What kinds of businesses could this apply to?

For example, food.

Let's say you make delicious homemade bread, or perhaps you know someone who does. Why not set up an online shop to sell these goodies? Customers can order online and pick them up in person or deliver them.

Even real estate properties. Think about the real estate industry. If you're a real estate agent or you know one who is looking to expand their client base, you could benefit from leveraging the internet. Instead of relying solely on walk-ins or referrals, you can use the power of online marketing to reach potential clients.

Here's how it works: you promote the properties online through targeted ads, enticing potential buyers with beautiful images and compelling descriptions of the properties. The goal is to prompt interested parties to leave their contact details for an appointment to view the property.

It's an intelligent way to automate lead generation and reach a wider audience, all with minimal effort.

Partnering with Offline Businesses:

Don't own an offline business?

No problem. Consider partnering with an offline business owner who could use a hand getting online. You could help them set up an online presence and share profits from any online sales. It's a win-win scenario - they get to expand their customer base, and you get a slice of the pie.

Marketing an offline business online doesn't need to be complicated, either.

If you're selling a simple product like homemade bread, you can start with a social media page and share your delicious creations.

This business model can offer a fantastic opportunity, mainly because competition tends to be lower. For instance, consider how many people in your local area are selling homemade bread online. Or how many real estate agents genuinely know how to leverage the Internet to get leads?

I've coined this business model as the "localized online business." You're marketing offline businesses online while maintaining that local touch and rapport with your customers.

So, are you ready to be the bridge that connects offline businesses to the vast world of online opportunities?

Idea #4: Content Creation and Monetization Via Ads

Want to make money while expressing your creativity and connecting with others?

Then content creation might be just the thing for you. It's an exciting opportunity to share your knowledge, experiences, and insights with the world while also earning some money.

So, what is content creation all about?

Well, it's about producing valuable content that people want to consume.

For instance, you could start a free newsletter if you love writing.

You can share about anything you're passionate about. It could be about cooking, personal finance, fitness, or even caring for pets. The key is to deliver value to your readers consistently. Once you've built up a subscriber base, you can earn by including sponsored ads in your newsletter.

Each time you send out a newsletter, you get paid.

I'm going to give you four pieces of advice when it comes to publishing a newsletter, so let's assume your niche is minimalist living...

Understand Your Minimalist Audience:

Before you begin, it's crucial to understand the interests and needs of your target audience. People interested in minimalism often seek simplicity, organization, and mindful living. They may be interested in tips on decluttering, minimalist design, and how to live a more fulfilling life with less. Understanding these needs will guide the content of your newsletter.

Provide Consistent Value:

Your newsletter should provide consistent value to your readers. You could share tips on how to live minimally, personal experiences or stories related to minimalism, product recommendations for minimalist designs, or news and trends in the minimalist world. The key is to deliver content that your readers find insightful and valuable.

Simplicity in Design:

Your newsletter design should reflect your audience's interest in minimalism. Opt for a clean, simple design that's easy to read. Use images sparingly and effectively, possibly showcasing minimalist designs or before-and-after decluttering pictures. Also, ensure your newsletter is mobile-friendly, as many of your readers will likely read it on their phones.

Promote Your Minimalist Newsletter:

Use your existing channels, such as your social media platforms, to promote your newsletter. You might also consider collaborating with other minimalist influencers to reach a larger audience. If you're starting from scratch, join online communities and forums where people interested in minimalism gather. Websites like Reddit have communities like r/minimalism, where you can engage in discussions, provide value, and subtly promote your newsletter.

Not a fan of writing? No problem.

Video content is super popular these days. You could create videos and share them on platforms like YouTube. Once your channel attracts viewers, you could earn revenue from ads displayed in your videos or sponsored content.

And if video is still not your preference, interview others in audio. That's podcasting.

Here are some steps to kickstart your journey as a content creator:

Step 1: Pick Your Niche

What are you passionate about? What do you enjoy talking about? What do you have expertise in? These are some questions that can help you find your niche.

Step 2: Research Trending Content

Next, spend some time researching trending content within your chosen niche. This will give you an idea of what people are interested in and help you develop content ideas. You can use tools like Google Trends or check out popular hashtags on social media platforms to get an idea.

Step 3: Create Quality Content

This is where the magic happens. It's time to create content that resonates with your target audience. Remember, it's not about quantity but quality. Aim to create content that educates, entertains, or inspires your audience. If your content doesn't provide any value to the viewer, then it's not good content.

An inspiring video is one that stimulates or arouses the viewer's emotions, motivates them, or prompts them to think differently. It could be a video sharing a powerful personal story of overcoming adversity. This social experiment sheds light on societal issues or a motivational talk encouraging viewers to pursue their dreams.

For example, let's say you started a health and fitness YouTube channel. An inspiring video could be a 'transformation' video where you share a personal journey from being unhealthy to achieving your fitness goals. You could include clips from your workouts, share diet tips, and talk about the mental challenges you faced along the way. This type of content inspires your viewers to take control of their health and builds a strong connection with them as you share a personal and relatable story.

A real-life example of a viral homemade video within a specific niche is the "Dad, How do I?" YouTube channel.

It was started by Rob Kenney, who grew up without a father figure and wanted to create a resource for others who might be in the same situation.

The videos are simple, often shot in Rob's garage or yard, and feature him explaining how to perform various tasks that a father might typically teach their child - from tying a tie to fixing a leaky faucet. The content is educational, providing practical skills, but it's also profoundly touching because of the backstory and Kenney's sincere desire to help others.

His channel quickly went viral, amassing millions of views and subscribers, as people resonated with his unique mix of practical advice and heartfelt sentiment.

The key to creating successful content is always to keep your audience in mind.

Think about their needs, interests, and challenges, and aim to create content that provides value in some way, whether that's through education, entertainment, or inspiration.

Authenticity also plays a significant role. Don't be afraid to let your personality shine through your content. This helps to build a connection with your audience and sets you apart from others in your niche.

Step 4: Be Consistent

Consistency is vital in content creation. Make a content calendar and stick to it. This will keep your audience engaged and help you build a solid online presence.

Step 5: Share and Promote Your Content

Once your content is ready, share it far and wide. Use your social media channels, website, email list – any platform where your target audience hangs out.

Your ultimate goal? To build a large follower base and establish a strong brand. Advertisers love influencers with a large, engaged audience. And once you've established your brand, you'll find numerous ways to monetize it.

Take the famous YouTuber Mr. Beast, for example. He has built a massive audience and a strong brand, allowing him to monetize his channel in various ways, including through ads, sponsorships, and even his line of products.

In a more unconventional move, he launched his virtual restaurant chain, Mr. Beast Burger, in 2020. Rather than setting up physical locations, he partnered with existing restaurants to prepare his menu. Customers can order Mr. Beast Burger meals for delivery through various apps. It's a novel idea that leverages his massive fan base and has allowed him to earn a substantial income while also supporting local businesses.

Idea #5: Create Your Own Digital Product To Sell

Creating and selling your digital product is a fantastic way to earn income online. The beauty of this model is that you have complete control over your offering, and once created; it can continue to generate income with minimal ongoing effort.

Because in our increasingly digital world, there's a rising demand for knowledge-based products to solve problems.

An information product is a packaged piece of expertise, knowledge, or advice that can be sold and delivered online. It leverages your skills or experience, turning them into a product that others can learn from. The real beauty of an information product is in its scalability. You create it once, and it can be sold repeatedly.

Here's how you can get started:

Step 1: Choose Your Niche

Start with identifying your niche market, similar to the previous Ideas. What are you passionate about? What are you knowledgeable in? What problems can you solve? This could be anything from photography to personal finance. The key is to find a niche where you can provide value and where there's a demand for your insights.

Step 2: Define Your Offer

Once you've settled on your niche, the next step is to nail down precisely what solution your digital product offers. This isn't just about the product but how it can help your audience. Are you planning to teach coding to beginners? Are you going to provide a comprehensive guide to sustainable living? Or perhaps you want to share your unique approach to cooking?

Remember, a successful digital product is about solving a problem or meeting a need. It could be offering a solution to a particular problem, like 'how to become a proficient coder from scratch.' Alternatively, it could be a compilation of various tips and hacks, like '101 Cooking Hacks to Make Your Life Easier.

Your offer needs to be compelling, relevant, and provide real value. It should resonate with your audience and make them think, "Yes, this is exactly what I've been looking for!" Crafting a clear, appealing offer is the cornerstone of your digital product, so take the time to get it right.

Step 3: Set Up Your Platform

Now that you have your offer, it's time to set up your platform to sell and deliver your digital product. You'll need a website as your primary platform and a secure system to manage transactions. This might sound daunting, but don't worry - Several user-friendly platforms like Teachable, ClickFunnels, SamCart, or Kajabi can simplify this process. They provide all-in-one solutions for hosting, selling, and delivering digital products.

As part of this step, you'll need to create a sales letter or a Video Sales Letter (VSL) to convince potential customers about the value of your product. Here are some tips for creating an effective sales letter or VSL...

Sales Letter:

Capture Attention: Start with a compelling headline that grabs attention and sparks interest.

Identify the Problem: Clearly state the problem that your product solves.

Present Your Solution: Introduce your product as the solution to the problem.

Provide Proof: Use testimonials, case studies, or data to prove your solution works.

Call to Action: Finally, direct your readers to take action, such as purchasing your product or signing up for more information.

Video Sales Letter (VSL):

Engage: Open with an engaging statement or question to hook your audience.

Storytelling: Use storytelling to make a personal connection with your audience. Share your journey or a customer's success story.

Solution: Introduce your product and explain how it can help solve the problem.

Testimonials: Like in a written sales letter, provide testimonials or case studies as proof.

Call to Action: End with a strong call to action, guiding viewers on what to do next.

Once a purchase is made, customers should have immediate access to the product. This can be facilitated through a password-protected member area. The best part is that platforms like the ones mentioned above automate this process, so once it's set up, you won't need to send out products each time you make a sale manually.

Step 4: Attract Traffic

With your platform all setup, it's time to bring in potential customers. Imagine your website or product page as a store in a bustling digital city. Now, you need to guide people to your store. This is where traffic generation comes into play.

Think of traffic as two main highways leading to your digital store: one is the Paid Traffic Highway, and the other is the Organic Traffic Route.

Paid Traffic Highway is like a toll road. It's faster and more direct, but you must pay for it. This involves using platforms like Google Ads or Facebook Ads. These are akin to billboards along the highway, directing people straight to your store. As a beginner, focusing on mastering one platform first is good. Google and Facebook are great starting points as they have the highest traffic volume and robust ad platforms.

On the other hand, the Organic Traffic Route is more like a scenic road. It's free and can be incredibly rewarding, but it requires more effort and time. This includes tactics like content marketing, viral traffic, and social media promotion.

Once your product has proven to convert well, creating an affiliate program is an excellent organic traffic strategy. Here, other people will promote your product for you in return for a commission on each sale they generate. To make your affiliate program successful, consider these tips:

Offer Competitive Commissions: Provide a good percentage of each sale to incentivize your affiliates. For each sale generated, you can even let them earn more than you.

Provide Marketing Materials: Make it easy for your affiliates by providing them with ready-made marketing materials like banner ads, email swipes, and social media posts.

Stay In Touch: Regularly update your affiliates about new products, promotional events, and successful selling strategies.

Recognize and Reward: Acknowledge your top-performing affiliates to motivate them to continue promoting your products. You can even through an affiliate contest for the top performers.

Step 5: Optimize Conversion

Now, we're at the final step: optimizing your conversion rate. This means ensuring that the highest possible percentage of visitors to your site make a purchase.

A few key areas to review and track:

Sales Copy and Video Script: These are your primary tools to convince visitors about the value of your digital product. Are they compelling and persuasive? Do they clearly explain the benefits and address potential objections?

Paid Ads Clickthrough Rates: If you're using paid ads, examine how many people click on your ads and visit your product page. If the clickthrough rate is low, you might need to adjust your ad copy or target audience.

Sales Conversion from Paid Ads: Now, out of those who clicked, how many are making a purchase? If this number is low, your product page might need tweaking. The sales copy isn't compelling, or the price is too high.

Offer Presentation: How is your offer framed? Is it clear what the customer will receive and how it will benefit them?

Social Media Analytics: Review your engagement stats if you're using social media. Which posts are performing best? What kind of content is your audience responding to?

Sometimes, poor conversion isn't about your website or offer. It could be that you're marketing to a non-profitable niche. For example, you might face challenges if you're selling a high-priced course about debt reduction to an audience who's already in debt. Those who need your product the most may not have the financial means to purchase it.

Once your product converts successfully, you can think about upselling or cross-selling. These strategies involve offering your customers more or more expensive products after their initial purchase. But remember, only plan for upsells when your main product is already successful. It's like adding more delicious dishes to a meal only after ensuring the main course is tasty and satisfying.

Remember, conversion optimization is an ongoing process. Keep testing, refining, and improving.

Start Your Digital Product Business By Giving Away A Free Workshop:

I'd like to share a strategy that has worked wonders for me: conducting a free live workshop. This strategy works like a charm because it serves several purposes.

Firstly, it's a fantastic way to build a list of potential customers. People must register to attend your workshop so you get their contact details. This is an invaluable resource because it means you have a direct line to a group of people who are already interested in what you're offering.

Secondly, while the workshop is free, you can make money by selling the recordings after they have registered. This creates an additional revenue stream and gives people who couldn't attend (or want to revisit the material) a chance to gain the valuable knowledge you've shared. Even those who are attending might want to buy the recordings to re-watch.

Thirdly, conducting a workshop is a solid commitment to actually creating your digital product. It's a deadline that forces you to get your material together.

But the process doesn't end with the workshop. After it's over, you can take the content and polish it up. Add more modules, create an accompanying guide or workbook, or even establish a community group where your students can interact and learn from each other. Once you've enhanced it in these ways, your workshop can be transformed into a comprehensive course that you can sell online.

Think of it as creating a product and an entire learning experience.

But there's more. Once you have your attendees list and their contact information, you can follow up with them via email. This gives you the opportunity to promote your workshop recordings or even affiliate programs from other companies that offer digital products. Doing so can earn a commission on any sales made from your referrals.

In terms of packaging your recordings into an impressive course, there are several things you can do. First, ensure the video and audio quality are good. Next, break down your workshop into bite-sized sections or modules, each covering a specific topic. This makes it easier for your students to digest the information and keep track of their progress.

Add PDF summaries or transcripts for each section, so your students can review the content in a different format or at their own pace. You could also create quizzes or exercises for each module to help reinforce the learning.

Consider adding bonuses or additional resources related to your topic. This could be templates, checklists, or even interviews with experts in the field. All these extras add value to your course, making it more appealing to potential buyers.

Lastly, present your course professionally and attractively. This includes creating compelling sales copy for your course description and designing professional graphics for your course.

Do continue to do your own self-study for the steps to achieving any of the 5 ideas mentioned in this chapter. Plenty of tutorials and courses exist to help you with this.

You can start with free training on YouTube and podcasts to learn the STEPS and also STRATEGIES.

I've also created a Playlist called, Free Course on my YouTube channel, **https://youtube.com/patricchan.**

Then, invest in yourself with some reasonable courses. When you find the right experienced coach you are comfortable with, do some research and consider getting coaching – that's the fastest way to learning and mastering skills.

Seriously, trying to learn by going through all the mistakes will be too much work.

As you continue your exploration of the five business ideas, remember that all these ventures are designed to kick off as part-time endeavors.

It's a stepping stone, a bridge that takes you from your current job to your entrepreneurial dream.

Because entrepreneurship will allow you to earn more and quicker to fill up your 3 financial buckets.

And if you can earn more, it means you'll get to have bigger buckets!

Anyway, why is the emphasis on starting part-time?

Starting part-time is like going on a journey with a backpack instead of a huge suitcase. The backpack represents your part-time venture – it's lightweight, manageable, and gives you the flexibility to move swiftly. On the other hand, a full suitcase (a full-time venture) can slow you down, making it harder to change direction if you encounter a roadblock.

Let's be honest. Balancing a full-time job and a part-time business can feel like spinning plates. But just like any other worthwhile endeavor, entrepreneurship doesn't come easy.

Take the example of Sara Blakely. She started Spanx as a side business while selling fax machines full-time. She hustled in the early mornings and late evenings, steadily building her business. Today, Spanx is a billion-dollar company, and Blakely is one of the most successful self-made female billionaires.

Although we're not aiming to become billionaires or wanting to have huge ventures as such, the entrepreneurial mindset is the same, isn't it?

The initial stages of your part-time venture will be a learning curve.

Starting a business is a lot like planting a garden. The first time you do it, you might not know how much water each plant needs, how much sunlight they should get, or how much space each one requires. But as you go along, you learn. You figure out the idiosyncrasies of each plant; you learn what works and what doesn't, and with each passing season, your garden gets better. Similarly, your part-time business is all about learning, adapting, and growing.

Now, let me be clear about something here. When you start making some cash from this side gig, please don't rush out to splash it on a new fancy phone or a dinner at that posh place. Nope.

That's not what we're aiming for. You see, this extra money you're raking in? It's not fun money. It's growth money. It's the high-octane fuel that will turbocharge your business and send it rocketing to new heights. So, keep your eyes on the prize - That's how we turn this part-time gig into a big-time success later on.

So, when is it time to bid farewell to your 9-to-5 job and embrace entrepreneurship full-time?

A good rule of thumb is to wait until your part-time business generates at least the same income as your day job. Or ensure you've saved up a safety net of at least six months' worth of your salary with the confidence that you know you're on the right track.

In the end, successfully navigating this transition from part-time to full-time entrepreneurship boils down to the following:

Perseverance: Keep going, even when the going gets tough. It's a marathon, not a sprint.

Optimism: Stay positive and believe in your business. You're its biggest cheerleader.

Hard Work and Discipline: There's no substitute for putting in the hours and staying committed.

Starting a part-time online business is like raising a child. Initially, you have this tiny, fragile entity that needs constant care and attention. It wakes you up at all hours, and sometimes it can feel like all you're doing is trying to keep it alive. But as time passes, you nurture, guide, and help it grow. You teach it to stand independently, make the right decisions, and grow stronger daily. Your business is like that child; you're the parent, guiding it from infancy to maturity. Sure, there will be growing pains along the way, but the joy of seeing it stand on its own and thrive makes it all worthwhile.

So, embrace the process, learn from your mistakes, and keep moving forward. Every step, every stumble, every victory is part of your entrepreneurial story.

At the same time, remember the earlier chapter about choosing your side hustle?

Now that you understand the 5 ideas, your side hustle should be related to the online business you want to start.

For instance…

Suppose you want to be a content creator. Then you should start the side hustle related to video editing. This way, you get to practice your skill of creating attractive videos while getting paid.

Sometimes, you can think more creatively as well. If you want to start an eCommerce business, perhaps, you can apply to do part-time customer support for an eCommerce company.

This way, you'll accumulate all kinds of information – including customer inquiries and complaints.

Wouldn't that help you a lot when selling your own eCommerce products someday?

After all, whichever side hustles you want to do, there's always an income opportunity. Thus, you'll be more competent to pick one that pays you money and gives you free experience and education!

Now it's time to build a business with a team…

Building a Team for Your Business

When you start a business, you're working on it alone. You're the webpage creator, the customer support, the marketer, the email sender, and every other position available.

Usually, the output of your work and effort has a limit.

But once you've dialed it in, where you're generating some consistent income, you can explore ways to increase the output.

My expertise is not about becoming a CEO and running a corporation.

It's how to create systems so that I can work less but still earn significantly more.

So, my model won't be able to be applied to an 8-figure business. But it's likely for 6 figures and 7 figures because I've done it before.

The model is called Operation Zero Employees.

To give you some context...

I think we all want to start an online business because we want to enjoy the "internet lifestyle" and have the freedom we can enjoy.

To build online businesses that can generate leverage income so that we only need to work some of the time.

I work about 8 - 10 hours a week, with the weekends off. That's about 2 hours a day, and I usually work in the morning until lunchtime.

If that's your goal too, making a predictable income every month from the internet and having time with your family (and for yourself too), then this may be the model that's suitable for you too.

Throughout this book, I haven't truly shared my background and expertise in making money using the internet. You see, I've been in this business for 2 decades now (maybe more by the time you're reading this).

I started in 2003.

And by 2005, I was getting invitations to speak at seminars and conferences worldwide!

In 2005 and 2008, I've spoken in 11 countries, including the United States, Australia, China, and the UK, as an authority on internet marketing. To date, I've spoken in 12 countries.

But after 2008, I stopped traveling worldwide to speak because I decided to spend time with my firstborn baby.

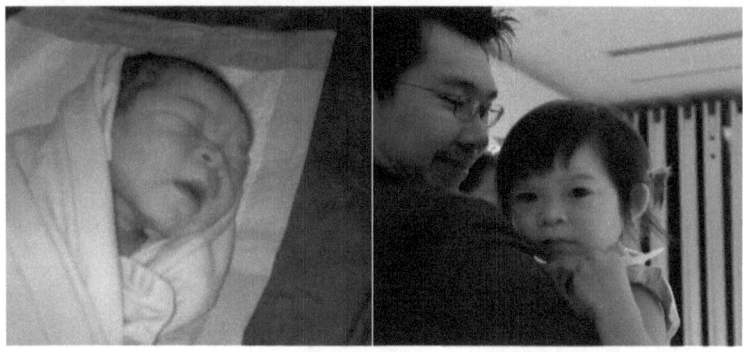

In 2013, I launched my online business seriously in ClickBank and achieved Platinum status after that. Since then, I've received the ClickBank Platinum Award for multiple years - an award only the 1% of ClickBank seller gets.

Combining offline and online, many of my students have made
millions using the internet. And it's common for some to make 5-
and 6-figure incomes.

Our product was even featured in Entrepreneur.com because it
helped my student achieve success, and they picked up her
success story.

My student's successes motivated me to write three best-selling
books about internet marketing.

One was even co-authored with Robert G. Allen, the New York
Times best-selling author of One Minute Millionaire, Multiple
Streams of Income, and many other mega-big bestsellers and
sold millions.

BUT what if I would tell you that...

I did all these with zero employees and only worked about 10
hours a week.

Because I build a business that makes money as passively as
humanly possible and, more importantly, gives me freedom.
To achieve this, I use a different approach:

"How can you generate more profit while scaling the business smaller?"

After all, the smaller the operation, the less overwhelmed you'll get; you'll also be making more money.

Simple science.

That's how "Operation Zero Employees" operates.
Before you continue reading, just let me get it straight –

If you want to build a $100 million startup or become a CEO working in a big office space, this is not for you.

This is for those who want to run and own an internet business with total freedom – without the baggage of managing employees, without going to the office every day, without having an HR dept, without having high overhead costs, without renting big offices, etc. You get the idea.

It's for someone who wants to make 5 to 6 figures of monthly income yet be able to work in Starbucks on their terms.

I mean, it doesn't have to be Starbucks – it could be in your preferred place to work. If you like, you could work in any country for that matter!

Basically, it's for someone who doesn't want to be controlled by a boss or even investors.

You can do whatever you want with your business - because you have the freedom NOW.

It all boils down to having a system.

After "testing" this model for five years before release, I can streamline the formula into 3 core components for you to create predictable incomes...

1. Operation
2. Automation
3. Campaign

And three of these are interconnected to become a SYSTEM to help build an evergreen online business without even needing you to have your own products to sell.

But in this chapter, I want to cover a part of Operation: having your team.

Having a team doesn't means you need to have employees.

In my company, all my team members have the right to do their own side hustles. Although they're still getting paid monthly, they're not my employees. Thus, it's "Operation Zero Employees".

In order to build your team, you need to shift your concept.

You're not looking for employees. You're looking for others who you can also help to achieve their goals.

It's a paradigm shift.

When I embraced this paradigm shift, my world changed. It gave me freedom, attracted the right people to me, and, more importantly, I knew I was doing the right thing because I was helping others.

With that concept in mind, you'll be able to approach others where you're helping them instead of trying to get them to work for you.

And in my online entrepreneurship journey, I've discovered that four leading roles need to be filled in any "operation" - the Mechanic, the Artist, the Manager, and the Entrepreneur. Each plays a crucial part in the success of the business.

The Mechanist: This is the person who usually takes care of the technical task. They typically have little creativity, as in they perform best when given the exact instructions to execute.

Some tasks under the Mechanist's belt in various online business models could include setting up stores, integrating your payment gateway, ensuring your website operates smoothly, scheduling your social media posts, setting up upsell funnels, creating member are for customers to access, etc.

The Artist: This is the creative soul in your team. Whether crafting beautiful designs, writing compelling copy, or brainstorming innovative solutions, the Artist brings a unique creative flair to your business. And sometimes, they can do the work better than you (unless you're also another Artist).

The tasks? They could include designing media for you, enhancing your video to look more attractive, writing your sales letter, etc – so long the work requires creativity.

Usually, their work is different from time to time because "art" is not always the same.

The Manager is the one who holds everything together. They're like the car's driver, ensuring everything is running smoothly and heading in the right direction. They coordinate, and they organize. They ensure that the Mechanist's work aligns with the Artist's creativity and that all of it fits into the Entrepreneur's strategy. Their strengths lie in their organizational skills and their ability to see to follow up with other team members ensuring they are not slack off.

Because your team is remote, having someone in charge of the entire team is critical.

The Entrepreneur: The visionary and leader of the team, your role is to steer the ship. If the Entrepreneur is you, you set the course for the business, make significant decisions, and inspire your team toward your shared goals.

You need to figure out…

Why are we doing this? Why will this work? Why is this better? What should we do?

They are also the ones who are constantly looking for opportunities for growth and expansion.

At the same time, keep in mind that the Entrepreneur is the one who funds the entire business. So, in other words, the business risk is always on the Entrepreneur.

Now, a single person can play multiple roles, especially in a small start-up, but ultimately, you want to build a team where these roles are filled by individuals who are best suited for them.

The trick is that you need to know where you are weak at. Then find a team member to fill in that vacuum.

And you may be wondering where I could find them?

Some of my team members have been with me for five years and even more than ten years.

Because with Operation Zero Employees Model, I do not restrict their side hustles, and we are all working remotely. This means they don't need to start work at 9.00 AM; they can choose their working hours. Likely, they don't see working in my company as a job but as a side hustle of their own.

For me, I don't "care" how many hours they work; all that counts is the output and KPI – end of the day, did the work get taken care of?

That's all that's relevant to me.

Here are some of the key places where I found my team:

Previous Employees: If you used to have a company or if you're running a business, you can always ask your previous employees to join you again. You could approach a prior employee with a job and get them to be part of your team.

Neighbours: Yes, it's true. I've managed to get my neighbours to be part of my team. If you've never asked, you'll never know. A neighbor could be a woman who is a mother and has some great talents, but she prefers to be a homemaker. You could offer her flexible work hours to help with some tasks for your business. Or a student. My team has students who are very good with computers, like social media editing and videos. And they're my neighbours too.

Referrals: This is how I found my programmer for my previous SaaS software platform business. It all started when I started a conversation with someone at a party, and they knew someone who could do programming. Then we set up a virtual interview and hired him. The programmer works from home, using the same Operation Zero Employees Model.

Freelance Websites: You can hire people from Fiverr or other freelance websites. Although I don't usually use this for hiring a team member, mostly for ad-hoc tasks, the reason is that for the team, these are people I know as a person, not just via email or picture.

I want you to think of it this way:

It's like employees working together in a company where they're not "freelancers". The difference is that the conventional employment rules and regulations do not restrict them, yet they get compensated with fixed monthly fees and can do anything else they want.

The advance that I have?

Flexibility and freedom. In my book, that's enough to be worth everything when running a business.

The C.A.M.P Formula

Once you find your team members, you need to build your team systematically. Here are the steps I use, which I call the 'CAMP' formula, and work the acronym backward:

C - Communication: You need a project management platform to communicate well with your team. There are plenty of options today, including Asana and Monday, but I'm currently using Basecamp because I started very long ago. And since everything is already archived there, it's too much work even to consider moving to other platforms.

And then, we use WhatsApp for any immediate communication needed. Other platforms would be Gmail and Zoom for regular meetings with the entire team.

A - Archive: There should be a master archive place for all your team members to look for the needed information. Archive all your training, SOPs, emails, and communication in a place like Google Drive or OneDrive. This is also why we'll always use a project management platform instead of communicating in Gmails – we want to archive everything for future reference.

M - Mechanical Work: In theory, mechanical work should be done by your team because they're not the "money makers" and with proper SOPs, a Mechanist should be able to do it.

So make sure to plan out all of the Mechanical Work so that your involvement is very minimal. This includes standard customer support, setting up Zoom classes, transcripts, and other tasks.

For instance, it has been years since I checked customer support emails or logged in to our helpdesk ticket center. The other reason is that it's an unavoidable fact that there will be haters or horrible customers from time to time. No matter how unreasonable they are, the truth is, I'll still get emotional with their statements and judgments.

So, why would I bother to be burdened with those despite their unreasonableness? I'll let my team take care of those.

P - Product Training: Regardless of what business models you're using, your business should have products. Your team members need to undergo product training to support them. Allow them to access your products, even if they're not free.

I'm not suggesting you do the same, but my team even gets to access my expensive training that sells for thousands of dollars.

Well, there are two aspects to this:

I would instead give that so that I don't need to work.

Secondly, with ZE Model, my mindset is a bit different. I'm always rooting for my team to achieve their own entrepreneurial success too.

As I've mentioned, my team members have their own side hustles, and some may have even generated more income than what they're earning from my company each month.

But I'm not afraid of losing them – because if they don't see the value of working with me anymore, they shouldn't.

However, the risk of losing them is minimal because I'm always striving to make it worth their time and effort to continue working with me.

The point is to build a system on which the operation, automation, and campaign are all focused. Your online business doesn't mean you must use the internet to find people. Start sharing offline, and you'll find your dream team.

So, there you go. That's how I find my team and operate with them. The same method can be applied to you. The key is to start talking and telling people what you need. You'll be surprised at how many people are out there who can help you with your business.

If you like to know more about Operation Zero Employees, check out https://operationzeroemployees.com

The Power of Starting Early: A Journey of Growth, Mistakes, and Compounding

Looking back at my journey, I sometimes kick myself for not starting earlier.

If I knew then what I know now about investing, I would have been miles ahead in my financial journey. But alas, wisdom often comes with time and experience, and the best thing we can do is share these lessons with those at the start of their journey.

Let's talk about starting early. Starting early in investment isn't just about putting money into some stocks or bonds while you're still in your 20s.

It's about these two things: acquiring knowledge and gaining experience through making mistakes.

Think of it as learning a new language. When you first start, you're an absolute beginner. You struggle with pronunciation, stumble over grammar, and can barely string together a simple sentence. But as you practice, you start to understand the nuances and the sentence structure. You make many mistakes, mispronounce words, and use the wrong verb tense, but you learn from those mistakes. Eventually, you become fluent, converse effortlessly, and understand complex texts.

Investing is no different. When you start early, it's like being a beginner in a new language. You might make some mistakes initially, pick the wrong stocks, or sell at the wrong time. But every mistake is a lesson in disguise, and every lesson makes you a more fluent 'speaker' in the language of investing. The earlier you start, the more time you have to learn, make mistakes, and become proficient investors.

Starting early also fosters financial discipline. It's like signing up for a marathon. You start training months in advance, gradually building up your stamina. You can't slack off or skip training sessions because you know that every bit of effort you put in now will determine your performance on race day. Similarly, when you start investing early, you commit to regularly setting aside a part of your income, cultivating discipline.

The other benefit of starting early is that it allows you to take more risks. As the saying goes, "Fortune favors the bold."

When you're younger, you can afford to invest in high-risk, high-return assets like stocks or cryptos because you have more time to recover from any potential losses. This won't be the case if you start investing later in life when your risk tolerance is lower, right?

Let's talk about Elon Musk's story, although it's not about investment but entrepreneurship. His story is an excellent example of someone who lost a lot early in his career but bounced back quickly because of his age, determination, and perseverance.

As you probably know, Elon Musk is known as the CEO of SpaceX and Tesla, but his journey to success was filled with many failures and losses.

In the late 1990s, after selling his first company, Zip2, Musk launched an online payment company called X.com. Despite initial success, the company faced fierce competition and was on the verge of bankruptcy. In 2001, Musk was ousted from his CEO position. He was devastated, and his professional future seemed uncertain.

But because he was still in his early 30s, Musk had time on his side. He took this failure as a learning experience and didn't lose heart. He knew he had the energy, time, and determination to start over.

In 2002, X.com was rebranded as PayPal and sold to eBay for $1.5 billion. Musk, as the largest shareholder, walked away with $165 million. Instead of retiring, Musk took his earnings and reinvested them into his next ventures, SpaceX, Tesla, and SolarCity.

With SpaceX, Musk faced another series of failures. The first three rocket launches failed, and the company was on the brink of bankruptcy again. But in 2008, the fourth launch succeeded, and SpaceX won a $1.6 billion contract from NASA.

Today, Musk is one of the wealthiest people in the world, but he wouldn't have reached this point if he hadn't started early, taken risks, and learned from his failures. His story exemplifies the power of starting early in investment and entrepreneurship. Despite the losses and failures, he had the time to learn, adapt, and ultimately succeed.

The second reason to start early is the magic of compounding.

The earlier you start, the more time your investments have to grow and multiply. Even if you invest smaller amounts, starting early can lead to significant growth over time.

Let's put some numbers to it. Suppose you invest $100 monthly with an average annual return of 7%. If you start at age 20 and continue until age 40, you will have invested $24,000. But thanks to compounding, your investment would have grown to around $70,000.

Now, let's consider someone who starts at age 30 and invests the same amount until age 40. They would have invested $12,000, which would have grown to around $16,500. The ten-year head start results in a difference of over $50,000! Imagine the difference when you extend this to age 50 or 60.

The point here isn't to intimidate you or make you feel like it's too late if you didn't start in your early 20s. I didn't start in my 20s either.

Instead, it highlights the incredible power of starting early, whatever 'early' may mean for you.

So, the best time to start is now, whether you're 20, 30, 40, or even 50. Acquire the knowledge, make those mistakes, and let your investments grow and multiply. You, too, can reach your financial goals by starting early.

Just embrace the journey, and let the magic of starting early and compounding do their work. After all, there is always time to become the investor you might have been.

Investing in Ethereum and Other Key Cryptocurrencies

If you've been keeping up with financial news or any news, you've probably heard about Bitcoin. But Bitcoin isn't the only player in the game. There's another crypto heavyweight, which is Ethereum.

Before that, I need to clarify something before we go any further: I'm not giving you financial advice. I'm not saying you should rush out and buy a bunch of Ethereum. I'm saying that it's worth considering in your portfolio as a High-Risk Investment. It's worth understanding. It's worth exploring.

So, why Ethereum?

Ethereum is not just a cryptocurrency. It's a platform. It's a blockchain-based platform that developers can use to build and deploy decentralized applications (dApps).

In other words, Ethereum is a platform that brings blockchain to the masses, allowing developers to create applications that take advantage of blockchain technology. And Ether, the cryptocurrency that powers the Ethereum network, is what you buy when investing in Ethereum.

This is why Ethereum is a compelling investment. It's not just about the value of the Ether you're buying. It's about the potential of the Ethereum platform. As more and more developers build on Ethereum, the more valuable the platform - and by extension, Ether - becomes.

But don't take this as a sign to put all your eggs in the Ethereum basket. Crypto, like all investments, comes with risks. The crypto market is notoriously volatile. Prices can skyrocket one day and plummet the next. So, if you decide to invest, make sure it's money you can afford to lose.

I'm also sharing with Ethereum because it can generate interest, too; this is through staking.

In a geeky way of saying, staking is a process in which you validate transactions on a blockchain network. It's a bit like putting money in a bank term deposit. You agree to keep a certain amount of money (in this case, Ethereum) in a particular wallet for a period. In return, you earn interest on that amount.

In Ethereum's case, this process is part of its shift from proof-of-work (PoW) to proof-of-stake (PoS) consensus mechanism. This upgrade is known as Ethereum 2.0 or Eth2. In PoS, the more Ethereum you stake, the higher your chance of being chosen to validate transactions and earn rewards.

Here's a basic rundown of how Ethereum staking works:

Minimum Stake: To become a validator in the Ethereum 2.0 network, you must stake a minimum of 32 ETH. However, many platforms allow you to stake with less by pooling your ETH with other users.

Locking Up Your ETH: When you decide to stake your ETH, you must send them to a specific deposit contract. Once you've done this, your ETH will be locked up for a certain period. You won't be able to access or use them until the completion of the Ethereum 2.0 upgrade, which could take a few years.

Earning Rewards: Once you've staked your ETH, you can start earning rewards, which come in the form of additional ETH. The exact amount you make will depend on the total amount of ETH staked in the network. The annual percentage yield (APY) for staking ETH varies; it can change based on how many people are staking. But it's common to see about 5%.

With ETH, you're still earning while holding the crypto coin.

Of course, I'm not suggesting you buy ETH right after reading this chapter!

Because I wouldn't know what's the price at this exact moment.

Following the suggestion from this chapter, you should buy it when the price is low because your goal is to hold and invest for the long term.

I know it sounds like a redundant piece of advice, true?

No. People do buy when the price is going up. Because they're catching the wave, but when it's going up so that you can sell when it goes even higher. That's the general concept of trading to make money.

Now, let's talk about other cryptocurrencies. Ethereum might be the second biggest crypto by market cap, but it's far from the only one worth considering. There are thousands of cryptocurrencies, each with unique features and uses. So, how do you pick the right ones to invest in?

Here are some bullet points to guide your research:

Purpose: What problem does cryptocurrency solve? Does it offer a unique solution or just a clone of another crypto?

Team: Who's behind the crypto? Do they have a track record of success? Are they transparent and active in the crypto community?

Adoption: Is the crypto being used in the real world? Are businesses or consumers using it for its intended purpose?

Security: How secure is the crypto? Have third parties audited it? Has it ever been hacked?

Regulation: Is the crypto compliant with regulations? Is it at risk of being banned or restricted?

Diversification is critical to managing risk in your investment portfolio, but you don't need too many. Crypto can be a part of that portfolio, but it shouldn't be the whole thing.

Here's an example, taking Binance Coin (BNB) to illustrate:

Purpose:

Originally, BNB was born to cover fees on Binance, which is, by the way, one of the biggest crypto exchanges out there. But, as it turns out, BNB had bigger dreams. Now you'll find it popping up in e-commerce, payment services, and more. And guess what? BNB is also the homegrown star of Binance's own blockchain, the Binance Smart Chain.

Team:

The team behind BNB? At the helm is Changpeng Zhao, or CZ, as he's known in the crypto world. CZ is pretty much a crypto celebrity, known for his straight talk and dedication to the crypto cause. He and the rest of the team have been instrumental in making Binance and BNB what they are today.

Adoption:

When it comes to adoption, BNB is killing it. Thanks to its integration with the Binance exchange, it's got a fan base of millions worldwide. And the fun doesn't stop there. BNB has been stepping out, making its mark in e-commerce and payment processing, including the NFT marketplace. Plus, with the rise of the Binance Smart Chain and its pocket-friendly fees and speedy transactions, BNB has become a hot favorite, especially for DeFi apps.

Security:

Now, you might be wondering about security. Well, being the poster child of Binance, BNB has a pretty tight security setup. But, like anything in the digital world, it's not immune to risks like hacking and price swings.

Regulation:

As for regulation, Binance, being the big player it is, is under the microscope of regulators worldwide. This is probably the only concern we'll have in terms of the stability of BNB as an investment. But as the rules of the crypto game continue to evolve, Binance and BNB will be adapting to the rules.

Understanding these 5 points help you better decide on what other crypto coins are worth exploring, other than Bitcoin and Ethereum.

I DO NOT buy "potential" crypto for investment — for instance, Memes Coins.

This is my opinion; I don't want all of these "Crypto Gurus" who are peddling their courses and coaching to be offended.

Because they are primarily by luck, yes, some people earned 10X... 100X and some crazy story.

But for each inspiring story like that, there are probably uncountable ones of those who lose money.

This book, MONEY: Present and Future, is about being smart with your money. I don't suggest using luck as part of your plan to become debt-free and achieve financial independence.

True story:

In the past, I've bought ETH for just about $200. But because I don't see it as an investment, I sold them off during the bear market, with the worry of losing money when it's plummeting.

But after that bearish period, ETH went up to almost $3,000. I would have earned over 10X return if I was still holding it. I failed to keep it because I wasn't thinking of an investor.

There's a difference between buying crypto for investment and trying to make some quick money.

I'm only proposing buying for investment – to hold for many years.

If you can't hold for years, I wouldn't suggest adding this portfolio at all.

Money: Present and Future –
Embarking on Your Financial Journey

Throughout this book, we've ventured together on a journey through the present and future of money.

We've explored various topics, from understanding the principles of personal finance, including "money traps" and the potential of investments, to the importance of starting early and diversifying our income streams.

We've also delved into the fascinating world of online business, examining various models and strategies that can provide the freedom and flexibility many of us seek in our lives. And we've done all this with the ultimate goal in mind - empowering ourselves to take control of our financial future.

Yet, this book is merely the commencement of a larger journey. It's your launch pad toward a voyage of continuous learning and financial growth.

It's a stepping stone on your financial independence and debt-free journey. And as with any journey, you'll need to keep learning and growing.

Here's a checklist to help you move forward:

- Review each chapter and note down the key takeaways.

- Set clear, achievable financial goals based on what you've learned.

- Embrace the power of small beginnings and early starts.

- Consider various income streams - remember the importance of diversification into your three buckets.

- Begin a side hustle. This can be a valuable way to gain experience in an area you're interested in while earning extra cash. Consider something that aligns with your long-term goals.

- Online business is the ideal way to earn faster; pick a model that suits you and learn more about it.

- Stay informed about financial developments, especially in the dynamic sphere of cryptocurrency.

- Be prepared to make mistakes and learn from them. Mistakes are inevitable, especially when you're trying something new. Use them as opportunities for learning and improvement.

- Remember to keep a balance - while money is important, it isn't everything.

And as you move forward, I want to emphasize one crucial point…

Maintain Your Learning Momentum:

The financial landscape is expansive and perpetually evolving. This book serves as a playbook, guiding you through the initial stages of your journey. But the learning shouldn't stop here. Numerous resources exist - books, e-courses, workshops, mentors - all with knowledge waiting to be tapped.

Make careful choices about who you learn from. Seek out those who are not only knowledgeable but also genuine and passionate about sharing their wisdom. Whether that's me or other Gurus, the important thing is the value they bring to your learning journey and the sincerity behind their guidance.

Parting Thoughts:

As we wrap up this book, I want you to remember that financial independence isn't merely about amassing wealth or having a hefty bank account. It's about achieving freedom - **the liberty to make choices, to share moments with those we cherish, to pursue our passions, and to make a positive impact on the world.**

Remember, money is a tool, a means to an end, not the end itself. Use it to build the life you envision, to open doors of opportunity, and to effect change.

When I wrote this book, my children were still young – Reeve is 9, Marireis is 13, and Marin is 15. They are the core motivation of why I want to be financially free and debt free to be with them.

So, take a deep breath and step into the fascinating world of personal finance. Seize control of your financial future and carve out your path. And don't forget to enjoy the journey. Because in the end, it's not just about the destination but the experiences you gather, the growth you witness, and the person you evolve into along the way.

Much love,

- Patric

P.S: If you wish to connect with me, my personal Facebook profile is facebook.com/patricchan

Where You Can Get More Education From Me

The Random Money Advice Newsletter

While I've included four chapters here, I will be releasing new Random Money Advice from time to time.

Or some additional highlights I may have from this book. Simply because there will always be new ideas or experiences I've gained along the way, and I would wish to share them with you. To subscribe for free, go to:

www.moneypresentandfuture.com

The NFTs for Creators Newsletter

I only wrote about NFTs in this book because this subject is very dynamic. I do not want what is written in this book to be obsolete. At the same time, I have nothing to teach about buying NFTs for speculations (which I discourage); what I'm teaching is creating your own NFTs as a Creator and serving your customers. To learn more, you can register for the NFTs for Creators Newsletter for free here:

patricnft.com/newsletter

Operation Zero Employees (ZE)

When building a digital business, the ZE model and philosophy will embody all of my training and teachings. ZE stands for "Zero Employees". It creates freedom for creators, digital marketers, influencers, and online entrepreneurs while empowering the "employees" to be independent and become bosses of their own businesses or side hustles. If you would like to learn more about it, visit:

zeroemployees.com

Hundreds Of Video Training For Free

There are hundreds of videos I've released on my social media. Some are short content, while there is also full-length training.

Frankly, the best thing you can do is to follow to receive future ones for free:

Facebook Page: fb.com/patricchanlive

YouTube Channel: youtube.com/patricchan

To Reach Me

If you're interested in engaging me as a speaker for your seminar/event or coaching, feel free to email me with your details at:

personal@patricchan.name

Our office WhatsApp number is +6012-2444 820.